How to Bass Fish Like a Pro

Copyright © 2012, John E. Phillips

D0100318

Table of Contents

Introduction

To be the best bass fisherman you can be, then you need to learn from the top bassers. Each bass fisherman has his favorite technique, his proven way of dealing with a problem and his best-producing lures. Therefore, I believe that one of the best ways you can learn about great bass fishing is to talk to more than one authority, and you will pick up tips from each one. That's the reason we've interviewed some of the best professional bass fishermen in the nation and let them tell you how they solve problems, choose lures and make the decisions they do before, during and after they go fishing.

Only in recent years, have we begun to study and learn that the emotions of fishing can and do play a major role in the success each angler has when he goes on the water to do battle with the bass. In this first book of our bass-fishing series, we've asked the pros about how they mentally approach a bass-fishing tournament, and how they rebound from losses.

Many years ago, back in the early days of BASS, I interviewed four of the nation's top bass pros. I asked them what would cause them to lose this tournament, and what would cause them to win this tournament. Each angler to the man predicted why he would lose the tournament, and Rick Clunn predicted why he would win it. Clunn said, "I just finished a tournament the day before I arrived for practice day at the Bassmaster's Classic. All my fishing techniques are working the very best they possibly can work. I am conditioned to the hot weather, and I believe this will be my best tournament ever." True to his prediction Clunn produced one of the best Bassmaster's Classics he ever fished in and won. Each angler who told me what would cause him not to win didn't win the Classic for the exact reasons they had predicted. I learned from that set of interviews that the angler's mental attitude plays a much-bigger role in his success or failure each day he goes fishing than I ever had believed.

I am often asked, "John, why do you write about other people and not put your thoughts or ideas in most of your books?" The reason is quite simple. From the time I first started writing, I decided I'd use my writing and my cameras to learn all I could about the outdoors from the very-best outdoorsmen I could find. And, as I learned better techniques and strategies and about better equipment, I would pass on what I had learned to the readers straight from the horses' mouths (the experts I interviewed) instead of taking that knowledge and packaging it under my name. A majority of the knowledge we learn in our lifetime comes from other people, and I prefer to share their knowledge as the expert rather than trying to be an expert myself. At one of the first writers' meeting I ever attended, a wise writer, who had been writing about the outdoors for more than 50 years, said, "Boy, you can choose one of two career paths; you can either write about the experts, or you can try to be the expert. But if you notice, the people who try to be the experts don't last nearly as long in our profession as the individuals who try to find the experts and write about them."

I've always found this advice to be absolutely on-target, and I have tried to follow it throughout my career. In this book, I've found the experts on bass fishing to enable you to learn from them as I have.

Chapter 1 - Kevin VanDam's Secrets to Consistency in Bass Fishing

Editor's Note: Seven Bassmaster Angler-of-the-Year titles, four of those consecutively and back-to-back Bassmaster Classic Championships make Kevin VanDam of Kalamazoo, Michigan, one of the most-consistent bass anglers on the professional-bass-fishing circuit today. Here's what VanDam says about his secrets to consistency.

Love What You Do and Use Search Baits

When I asked Kevin VanDam what his secret was to always doing well in bass tournaments and consistently winning big tournaments and titles, VanDam answered, "I love what I do. I don't view anything about tournament fishing as work. When I wake-up in the morning to practice before a tournament, I'm totally aware that I'm one of the luckiest people I know, because I get to do what I truly love for a living. One of my strengths is fishing fast. I try to cover a lot of water quickly to find out where the bass are holding. For instance, Lake Guntersville in Alabama has a number of great places to fish, but not all those areas hold bass. So, I'll fish as fast as I can and locate as many bass as I can. Then when the tournament begins, I'll have plenty of productive spots to fish.

"I have three favorite search baits that I use. Each of those baits is designed to search a different depth of water for bass. For instance, I'll use the Strike King KVD 1.5 and 2.5 to locate bass in 1 to 2 feet of water and the Strike King Series 6XD to find bass in water depths of 30 feet. These lures allow me to search different depths of water to determine at which depth of water the bass are holding. And, I don't overlook the spinner bait. I can fish the Burner spinner bait right on the surface, and the Bottom Dweller spinner bait I can fish as deep as I want. I can fish all these spinner baits fast. I also use the Rodent and the Coffee Tube. I can flip those two at targets and hop them one time off the bottom. Remember that in practice I'm just looking for bass, not trying to catch every bass in the area or pick-apart the cover. I just want to know where the bass are holding, the water depth at which the bass are holding, the type of structure where they're holding, and the area of the lake that's holding the most bass. I always can come back on a tournament day to pick-apart the cover and fish every piece of cover in that region."

VanDam told me that he never has seen a ledge he hasn't loved to fish for bass. He's known as a ledge fisherman and has won a number of tournaments and caught a lot of bass off ledges. I asked him how much research he does to pinpoint the ledges on the lakes he fishes, and he replied, "I don't get on the Internet and look for information. I look at a lake map to try to determine where the bass should be at the time of year when I'm fishing, under the weather and the water conditions I'm fishing. Then,

I study a topo map of the lake to see the ledges and the drop-offs that show-up on the map. I'll go one step further and graph the area, once I reach the lake. I use a Humminbird side-imaging unit, which is an unbelievable tool for fishing ledges. This unit gives me a detailed picture of not only what's underneath the boat, like most depth finders, but also what's off to the side of the boat. With a Humminbird side-imaging depth finder, I can look at about 200 feet of bottom at once, whereas with the old depth finders, I only could look at about 10 feet of bottom.

"Also, to locate the ledges, I spend a lot of time with crankbaits trying to cover the ledges and search for those little ledges that most people may not find. The obvious places, like points, main river drop-offs, creek-channel junctions and easy-to-find ledges probably have been found by every bass fisherman who fishes that lake and are fished really hard. So, I search for drop-offs and ledges that probably aren't on any lake maps. I'm looking for the very-subtle drop-offs, like a 1- or a 2-foot drop-off. I still won't find those hidden bottom breaks, unless I spend a lot of time cranking a crankbait. I can fish those shallow ledges that only may be 1-foot deep with the KVD 1.5 or 2.5 and those deep ledges more than 20-feet deep with a Series 6XD. The Series 6XD dives deeper than any-other crankbait, so I can find and fish the ledges other fishermen aren't able to fish with other crankbaits. These crankbaits give me a better picture of the bottom and enable me to feel the type of structure on the bottom.

4

"When I'm fishing a ledge, I try to let the bass tell me where they're holding on that ledge on that day. Where the bass are holding on a break on any given day depends on the amount of current coming to the lake from hydroelectric-power generation. In a fast current, the bass typically will pull-up on top of the ledge and to the most-shallow part of the ledge. On a slow current, the bass may be holding right on the break of the drop-off. With no current, the bass may be suspended off the edge of the break. I experiment with various crankbaits, running them at different depths to try to get a bite. When I get a bite, I'll know how the bass are positioned on that bottom break. Once I know where the bass are holding, I can position my boat to fish that water depth and select the crankbait designed to run at that water depth.

"I've learned that bass will change their holding positions often during the day. To consistently find and catch big bass on lakes with hydroelectric-power generation, I'll call the power company on those lakes to learn the power-generation schedule and know when they'll start pulling water and running current. Then, when the time comes close when the current's supposed to be running, I watch the sticks and the limbs that are sticking-out of the water to see if I can see the current moving. This tells me how I need to position my boat to fish for the bass on the ledges.

"Most bass fishermen will cast onto a shallow flat, bring their crankbaits over the lips of the breaks and then back to their boats. Or, they try to parallel that bottom break, so their lures are running right on the edges of the breaks. I'll sometimes put my boat on the shallow side of the drop-off, cast-out to the deep side and bring my crankbait from the deep water over the lip of the break and up to the shallow side of the break. I use this tactic when I'm fishing a bottom break I know is holding bass. I've learned that when I can show the bass my crankbaits coming from a different angle than they're accustomed to seeing, I can trigger a strike that I never will have gotten if I've continued to fish from the same direction from which I've fished earlier. Also, when I know the bass are inactive, I may change from a crankbait, cast a Football Jig out into the deep water and drag it from the deep water, up the ledge, over the top of the ledge and into the shallow water. Many times that action will elicit strikes that I may not have gotten with a crankbait. When you pinpoint a ledge where you know the bass are holding, oftentimes you'll have to vary the position of your boat, not just your lures and the types of retrieve you're using. To catch bass on a ledge, you may have to bring your bait from several-different directions to

find out which way the bass want to take the bait. That's one of my keys to consistency."

Fish a Finesse Worm

VanDam says that he knows that one of the reasons he's been consistently successful is that he's helped design the lures he fishes. When I asked him why he decided that the world needed a different finesse worm when there are so-many finesse worms on the market already, he explained,

"Strike King and I wanted to develop shapes and colors that made our soft-plastic lures better than any others on the market. But first we wanted our soft-plastic lures to have an edge. We wanted our soft-plastic lures to be constructed with better material than the material other companies used to make their soft-plastic lures. So, we came-up with a new type of plastic – the Perfect Plastic – for our finesse worms. We wanted a softer plastic with a heavy salt content to give the bait a good sink rate, especially when the worm was rigged wacky style. The salt also made the worm heavier than most finesse worms, allowing you to cast it without having to add weight to the worm or the hook. The tail on most straight-tailed worms (finesse worms) had no action. We wanted the Perfect Plastic Finesse Worm's tail to have action. The tail's flipping and moving, made this finesse worm very versatile, whether you were fishing it on a Carolina rig, a shaky-head jig or a Texas rig.

"I primarily fish the 7-inch 3X Elaztech Finesse Worm. Of course, that decision on what to fish depends on the lake I'm fishing. In tournaments, I fish for big bass. The 7-inch Finesse Worm gives me the properties and the actions of a finesse worm in a longer profile. When you say the words finesse worm, you usually think about a 4-1/2- or a 5-inch worm. However, if you can get the action and the finesse technique in a larger-size finesse worm, then you can attract larger bass. If I'm fishing a smallmouth lake, I'll choose a 5-inch KVD Perfect Plastic Finesse Worm. If I'm fishing a lake with a number of spotted bass, I'll use the smaller Finesse Worm. I'm not a one-lure fisherman. If I'll be fishing a Finesse Worm, I want it in my boat in several sizes to let the bass tell me which size they want to eat on the day I'm fishing. If they won't eat the 7-inch Finesse Worm, I'll present them with the 5-inch worm. However, when I'm targeting bigger bass, the 7-inch Finesse Worm is my lure of choice.

"I choose my lure colors based on water clarity, the amount of sunlight the water gets and the depth at which I'm fishing. But if I only can pick three Finesse Worm colors this is what I'd choose. If I only could pick one color to fish anywhere in the nation, more than likely I'll choose green pumpkin. But dirt-colored Finesse Worms are my favorite almost anywhere that I fish, if the water's clear or slightly stained. If the water's dirty, or I'm fishing in Florida, I prefer the junebug or the redbug color."

Don't Abandon the Spinner Bait for Bass

In years past, VanDam was known as the spinner-bait kid. However, in recent years, he seems to have abandoned the spinner bait to fish the crankbait. When we talked about why, he told me, "I fish the spinner bait a lot, depending on the conditions. Remember, the trendsetters in tackle usually come from the Bassmaster Elite Series Tournament circuit. The states, the rivers and the lakes where the tournaments are set-up have a lot to do with the types of lures I'll fish to catch the bass. For instance, we fish different lakes at various times of the year more now than we have in the past. The last few years, many of the Bassmaster Elite Series Tournaments have occurred after the spawn and in the summer months when the bass have moved offshore. Then we need to fish deeper than we do in the early spring and the early fall. So, when the bass are moving-out to deep water, the crankbait becomes the dominant lure I'll use to catch those post-spawn bass. Remember that during the first day of the 2011 Bassmaster Classic on the Louisiana Delta in February, the only bait I threw was a spinner bait. I catch tons of bass on a spinner bait all the time.

"The Burner spinner bait lets me fish really fast close to the surface of the water, and the Bottom Dweller allows me to get-down in deep water and crawl on the bottom. Much of my early success was with spinner baits, because the tournaments were held during the time of year that the spinner bait was the best tool to use. Those spinner baits still catch tons of bass. In the Bassmaster Elite Series Tournament on the Arkansas River in Little Rock, Arkansas, in June, 2011, I caught a number of bass on the spinner bait. One of the keys to my success at catching bass at any time of the year is being able to identify and use the best lure to find and catch the bass at the time of year and under the weather and the water conditions we have to fish in each tournament.

"So, I haven't abandoned the spinner bait, but because we're fishing more post-spawn tournaments, the crankbait has been a better tool for me out in deep and extremely-shallow water. Also, we fish a lot of lakes where many anglers fish spinner baits. To give the bass a different look, I'll fish a crankbait in a spot that others may say is a spinner-bait spot. By fishing a crankbait in that area, I'm able to present a lure to the bass that they may not have seen in that location for a long time. This difference in lures may generate strikes that I won't have gotten if I fish the spinner bait like everyone else. Too, I believe in changing the look of the spinner bait. At the Bassmaster Elite Series Tournament on West Point Lake in LaGrange, Georgia, in May of 2011, I caught a number of bass using the Baby Burner spinner bait. A spinner bait is much like a plastic worm. To consistently catch bass, you've always got to have a spinner bait tied-onto one of the rods on your casting deck.

"When it comes to favorite colors and weights of spinner baits, I use whatever size spinner bait fits the conditions I'm fishing on that day. At any time I'm practicing or fishing, I'll have at least 500-different spinner baits in my boat. I've got spinner baits from as little as the 1/4-ounce Burner to the 1-3/8-ounce Bottom Dweller. One of my favorite colors for clear-water situations is the blue shad, and I like the chartreuse sexy-shad color also,

especially if the water has a little stain or color to it. The number-one selling color spinner bait every year is chartreuse-and-white. But that chartreuse sexy-shad color is more productive for me than the standard chartreuse-and-white."

Use New Lures

When I mentioned to VanDam, that throughout the last 3 or 4 years, the one type of lure we rarely ever heard his name associated with was a top-water lure, he reported that, "I do fish top-water lures, especially when we go to the lakes that have a shad spawn. If we happen to be fishing a tournament on a lake that's having a shad spawn, you'll see me fishing top-water lures, just like the other pros. In the past, some anglers have had problems making a top-water bait perform the walk-the-dog-type action. I'm using a fairly-new bait, the Sexy Dog, that doesn't dive under the surface, and stays on top of the water, even in choppy water. This lure also has a great gliding action. It comes in a variety of colors. Of course, there will be a sexy-shad color and some natural and translucent colors. I like to use this lure during the post-spawn, and I really like to cast it around targets when the bass are holding on bushes and boat docks. Too, I like to fish it around grass beds.

"The Sexy Dog has a drawing ability to pull bass out of their hiding spots and cover. Of course, during the shad spawn in the spring and then when the bass spawn, this lure will be dynamite. Even when the bass pull-out of the shallow water and move-out onto the deep-water ledges, you'll be able to pull them up to the surface to take this bait. Too, when the bass move into the creeks in the fall and start schooling, this new lure will be hard to beat.

"I caught a number of bass at the Bassmaster Elite Series Tournament at Lake Murray in Columbia, South Carolina, in May a few years ago, when we had a blueback herring spawn. I cast the Sexy Dog off shallow rocky points and around schools of herring. One of the things that helps me in my fishing is I'm always looking for a new, a better or a more-efficient lure than what's in my tackle box. Because I'm fortunate enough to be able to help design most of the lures I fish with, I feel that when I'm not catching bass, I need a different lure that will help me start catching bass. So, every year, as focused as I am on catching more and bigger bass, I'm also focused on how to develop a lure that will help me catch more and bigger bass."

To learn more about Kevin VanDam and his fishing, go to www.kevinvandam.com.

Chapter 2 - Be a Guide Like James Niggemeyer to Become a Pro Fisherman

Editor's Note: For many years, James Niggemeyer of Van, Texas, has been a fishing guide on Texas' famous Lake Fork, which is known for historically producing large numbers of 10-pound-plus bass. Niggemeyer will tell us how being a bass-fishing guide has helped him become a professional fisherman.

Learning to Get Along with People

When I asked Niggemeyer what he had learned from being a professional-fishing guide that had helped him become a professional fisherman, he responded, "As a guide, I get to see and meet, as well as fish with, many different people from all over the country. When I'm guiding, I can learn different techniques of finding and catching bass from my clients. Some of the people I guide have shown me tactics for catching bass I've

never thought of using. So, as well as teaching them how, when and where to catch bass on Lake Fork where I guide, my clients have taught me techniques they've learned from the areas where they've fished. I've guided a lot of vacationing fishermen who have high-skill levels in bass fishing but aren't from Texas and have never been to Lake Fork before. But they want to go fishing and catch bass immediately. So, I have to find bass and then show them how to catch the bass quickly. The pressure of having to locate bass quickly and not only catch them but teach others how to catch them has made me a better fisherman. A guide experiences pressure to perform every day as a top-level bass fisherman. That's the same pressure we feel when we're tournament fishing. Therefore, the sooner you get accustomed to the pressure and learn how to deal with it, the better angler you'll become."

Dealing with Weather and Water Conditions

Niggemeyer says he's learned a lot from being a bass-fishing guide that has helped him as a tournament fisherman. "When people book a bass-fishing trip with a guide, they generally have a certain day they want to fish, and their entire schedule revolves around that date. That the lake is muddy, extremely clear, falling, rising or that the bass haven't been biting for a week are problems never taken into consideration for the day they want to fish. So, regardless of the fishing conditions, a bass-fishing guide is expected to find bass and help his clients catch bass. If you can't, your fishing-guide business won't last long. The same is true

of tournament fishing. Tournament schedules often are set-up a year in advance. Tournament directors don't know what the weather, the water or the wind conditions will be on that day, or what the tournament anglers will have to deal with when they reach a lake to start competing. As a tournament angler, if you've dealt with a wide variety of fishing conditions before you have to compete under those same conditions, then you have an advantage.

"As a guide, many times I've had to take clients out when the conditions haven't been right for catching bass. Even though I've told my clients the conditions aren't right, they've booked the trip and wanted to go whether the weather's rain, snow, sleet or shine. As I've mentioned, some of the fisherman I've taken on a guide trip have been really-good bass fishermen and willing to endure the elements to try to catch a big

bass. Having that background and experience have really served me well as I've come up through the ranks of bass-fishing club, regional and national tournaments. I've learned that on the day you're scheduled to fish, you go fishing and deal with the elements you have on that day."

Moving-Up the Ladder

I discussed with Niggemeyer how he moved from being a bass-fishing guide to being a Bassmaster Elite circuit angler, and he told me,

"Part of being a guide is getting to know and understand your equipment and the people who manufacture and sell that equipment. I'd been fishing out of a Bass Cat boat for several years, and a couple of years ago a Bass Cat owner's tournament was to be held on Norfolk Lake in Mountain Home, Arkansas. At that tournament, I met Chris Brown, who was representing Strike King, at a booth. I had the opportunity to talk with him. I asked Chris what type of program Strike King might have for a professional-fishing guide to be able to buy Strike King Lures, and what I could do to work with Strike King and begin to promote the company and their lures. Chris explained what I needed to do to become an entry-level Strike King fishing guide and how I could get involved in Strike King's regional guide program. That's how I started my relationship with the Strike King Company, which has resulted in my finally becoming a Strike King pro. One of the key elements to getting a sponsor is remembering that companies are looking for fishermen and guides who can help the company grow. They're not looking to give out products and money to anyone who hasn't helped the company. I wanted a chance to show the folks at Strike King what I could do for them."

Going from Fishing Guide to Sponsored National Pro

When I asked Niggemeyer what he did as a regional Strike King pro that helped him become a nationally-sponsored, professional fisherman for Strike King, he said, "I worked different shows and promotions for Strike King whenever the company asked, I spoke to bass clubs about how to fish Strike King lures, and most importantly, I was available to do whatever Strike King needed me to do. There are a lot of anglers out there who can catch bass, but Strike King wants its pros to not only catch bass, but also be able to teach other people how to catch bass with Strike King lures. I set-out not to just get Strike King lures at a reduced rate, but to prove that I could be a valuable asset to the Strike King Company. I got sponsors the same way I learned to become a tournament bass fisherman. I started out small, getting to know the people in the company, learning what they needed me to do to help the company and then did it.

"Too, I watched other professional bass fishermen on the Strike King Pro Staff to learn how they dealt with the public and the media and the types

of things they did for Strike King to prove their value. Then, I followed their examples. I went the same route I did as a tournament fisherman. I knew I wasn't a tournament pro when I first decided to try to become one. So, I learned all I could from everyone who would teach me anything, took my time and grew into the sport, rather than trying to jump into the sport. I wanted to be sponsored as a fishing guide by Strike King because I used the company's lures and bought them at full retail. As a fishing guide, you fish a lot of days during the year. If you catch bass on a certain lure, and your client doesn't have that lure, you have to let him use your lure. In many cases, my clients and I lost a lot of lures, and I had to buy more, which was quite a drain on my guiding business. So, it only made sense that I should look for sponsorship with the companies whose products I already used, believed in and knew would help me and my clients catch bass.

"As I progressed as a fisherman, I kept this same philosophy. I only approached companies that made products I used and believed in and people within those companies I had learned to trust. I also was interested in long-term relationships. I wanted to work with companies that I knew with people who knew me and would go through the ups and the downs of tournament fishing with me. I wanted to go with a company that would grow with me."

Living Your Bass-Fishing Dream

Niggemeyer says being a full-time sponsored national professional bass fisherman is, "A dream come true. I'm so humbled to be part of a team that includes names like Denny Brauer, Kevin VanDam, George Cochran, Mark Menendez, Greg Hackney and Shaw Grigsby. The guys on the Strike King professional-fishing team are legends in the sport. I've looked up to and read about many of these pros for most of my fishing career. To be a member of the Strike King Pro Staff with these other pros is a big honor for me. Too, these great pros have really been helpful to a newcomer like me. They're not only a great group of fishermen, but they're also a great group of individuals who want to see other bass fishermen succeed as much as they have. I'm very blessed, and as far as the future for me, I've set goals for myself that I hope to be able to accomplish. My number-one goal every year is to qualify for the Bassmaster Classic. Once you've been to the Classic as a competitor, nothing will quench the thirst of that type of competition, except competing again. My second goal is to win a Bassmaster Elite Series Tournament. These are the two biggest goals I have on my mind at the beginning of every fishing season. My third goal is to win an Angler-of-the-Year title and/or the Bassmaster Classic. I know those are big dreams, but those are the dreams of every Bassmaster Elite Series fisherman at the beginning of each and every season. I hope to continue as a professional fisherman as long as God's willing, and I'm in good health and can provide for my family. I want to continue as a professional fisherman as long as I can. I have a great life.

"I listened to my mom and dad, went to college and got a degree. But I wish instead of trying to become a professional fisherman right out of college that I had learned a craft, a trade or developed a business that could have helped pay for my fishing and could have become a job I could depend on, regardless of how I did in bass-fishing competitions. My mom and dad were wiser than I was when they told me to get a good job first, while continuing to pursue my dream as a bass fisherman, and to always have skills I could use. My advice to a young person would be to go to college, find a degree, get a good job and then pursue your bass-fishing dream."

To learn more about James Niggemeyer and his fishing, go to www.jamesniggemeyer.com.

Chapter 3 - Five Secrets to Becoming a Better Bass Fisherman with Mark Davis

Editor's Note: During 2010, professional angler Mark Davis of Mount Ida, Arkansas, reinvented himself and has emerged from his worst year ever of tournament fishing in 2009 as a better bass and tournament fisherman. Now, we'll learn Davis' five secrets to becoming a better bass fisherman.

Secret # 1 – The Importance of Mental and Tackle Preparation

Mark Davis explains that to become a better bass fisherman, "First, understand that each of the bass-fishing secrets I'll be giving here stands on the shoulders of the secret that has come before it. So, when we reach the final secret No. 5, you can see how the four secrets that have come first have prepared you for the final one. As we go through these secrets, remember that we're building a house with a solid foundation, then strong walls and finally, a secure roof that helps you to become the bass fisherman you want to be.

"The number-one secret to turning a bad bass-fishing season around, as simple as this may sound, is to take the time required to sit-down and organize your tackle. Think through each tournament you'll be fishing, and make sure you'll have the exact baits you'll need, when and where you'll need them. I know that idea sounds simple, but most guys want to be fishing, not getting their tackle ready to go fishing. If they have any days off, they prefer to fish rather than organize their tackle. But as a tournament fisherman, when I leave the house, I'll be fishing from Texas to California, New York, Florida and many of the states in-between. So, I have to sit down and think through each tournament scenario and organize my tackle accordingly. I may be on the road for 2- or 3-months before I return home. I have to organize my tackle, so I'll have the lures, the line, the rods, the reels and everything else I'll need for every tournament. Then I have to put-in the other lures I may need if the lures I've thought I'll need don't work. This tackle organization can take a lot of time, thought and preparation. You also have to think about other stuff you'll need, like a push pole or a sea anchor.

"After you've decided on the tackle you'll need, you have to pack it in a way that you'll know where it's located in your truck or boat. Then you can go straight to those places and get what you need. By doing this, you'll out-think and be better prepared than most fishermen. In most tournaments, many fishermen will take a wide variety of gear and lures with them and hope they have everything they need when they'll need it. They don't spend the time, the energy and the mental preparation to think through each fishing situation they may encounter on each lake to make sure they have the lures, the line, the rods and the reels they think they'll need and the back-up equipment and lures they may use, if their first-string tackle doesn't pay-off. Most professional anglers will tell you that bass fishing is more of a mental game than a physical game. So, to become a better bass fisherman, you have to spend plenty of time preparing mentally. You do this by thinking about the lake you'll be fishing and the lures you'll need, being certain not to overlook any other lures you may need. Before you leave home to go tournament fishing or fun fishing, spend the time required to think through that fishing trip, and organize your tackle and thoughts to be mentally and physically prepared for any water, wind and weather conditions you may face on that day. At the end of the week, you'll see how step one is the secret foundation upon which you build to become a better fisherman. One of the real disasters that happen to bass fishermen is when they get out on the water and decide there's a lure they need to get the bass to bite, but they don't have the lure with them. That one decision or lapse of preparation can cause you to go from a hero to a zero in bass fishing."

Secret #2 – You Can't Overlook Your Homework for Success on the Water

Mark Davis shares his #2 secret to have a successful bass-fishing tournament. "One of the major keys that helped me turn my career around during 2010 was researching the bodies of water I'd be fishing in the Bass Elite Series tournaments. By pre-fishing every lake that the Bassmaster Classic Elite Series fished this year, I was more prepared. I even flew out

to California for a refresher course well ahead of the tournament to look at the lakes we'd have to fish and made some notes of good ideas I thought might work when we went there for the tournament. This exercise helped me to prepare myself mentally and physically to fish these lakes. Leaving home, flying across the country, riding around on a couple of different lakes and spending 5 to 10 days looking at water and structure and trying to figure-out how I'll fish those areas before a tournament was expensive and time consuming. Scouting trips aren't cheap, especially when you go to places with which you're not that familiar. I went to several-different lakes I hadn't fished awhile. I got a good mental picture of the types of places I might want to fish and how to get around the lake. I looked at the possible fishing spots, learned the locations of the boat ramps and tried to determine the kinds of tactics that might work during the time of year we would be fishing there. I realized the weather and the water conditions would change as would the bass' seasonal migration patterns from the time I scouted to the time I fished there. But I had more confidence in my ability to find and catch bass after I scouted the lakes, than if I hadn't put in that time and money to get mentally and physically prepared for each lake we had to fish this year.

"I felt that scouting had really paid-off for me. I spent the money and the time to go to the California Delta, learn the lakes and get mentally prepared to fish them. I finished 16th in that tournament, but I easily could have had a top-10 finish there. I hadn't been to the California Delta in a number of years, especially on a research trip, and I realized that I'd forgotten a lot about this body of water. It took more than a week riding the lake to learn it. But when I came-away from the Delta, I had a good mental picture of this body of water and knew how I needed to fish it and the lures I probably would need to use. I went in the fall, but we didn't fish it until March. I couldn't have learned what I needed to know to perform at my best, if I'd only relied on the 2-1/2-days of practice before the tournament. Because of my research, I knew where the best grass could be found, where the better bass-fishing areas of the lake were located, and how to reach those areas. I found a place to stay, and because of all that preparation, I fished better than I would've fished if I hadn't spent the time, the energy and the money to do my homework."

Secret #3 – Make Your Bass-Fishing Practice Count

Davis explained to me as we talked that, "The third secret key to becoming a better bass fisherman and, more specifically, a better tournament bass fisherman is to make your practice days count before the tournament begins. Practice is when you actually find bass that you'll try to catch during the tournament. To be a successful fisherman and become a successful bass fisherman, you have to locate the bass before you can fish for them. Most people look at a bass-fishing trip as a time to find bass and catch them. But I've learned that catching bass is a two-step process with the first step being to locate them before you can catch them. If you're fishing in a tournament, you have to know where the bass are holding that

25

you want to catch before the tournament begins. Also, besides locating the bass, you have to be able to determine what the bass will be doing on the day you're fishing for them. Most of the time pre-determining what a bass will do is very difficult, but that's the most-important information to learn, if you'll be fishing a multi-day event. Knowing where the bass will go when they leave the spot where you've found them can be the difference between winning or losing a tournament or doing well or performing badly in a tournament.

"Learning the bass's movement patterns is important. We've already discussed how to prepare and organize your tackle, so you can fish with the best lures you have on the day you're fishing. Then, we've talked about scouting the lakes you'll be fishing, so you'll know where the bass should be and how to reach them. Now, we'll learn how those first two steps should result in bites, which will help you know where the bass are concentrated and help you identify their behavior patterns. I want to know if the bass are either concentrated in or moving to shallow or deep water, what lures they'll bite, the best tactics to catch these bass and the bass' spawning stage. This is critical information to learn on practice days, because if you know the bass are coming-off their beds and moving-out to deep water, you understand you need to get ahead of those bass to deep water. Then the bass will be coming-to you and not moving-away from you. If you don't make the most of those 2 practice days before a tournament, covering a lot of water and learning all you can about what the bass' behavior patterns are right now and where they should be in the next 2 or 3 days, more than likely you'll be totally lost on tournament days."

Secret #4 – The Importance of Making the Correct Decisions on the Water

Mark Davis emphasized that secret number four meant, "Whether you win or lose a tournament or catch bass on your day off or not, will be a result of the decisions you make on the day you fish. At the end of every day, most tournament fishermen will question where they've gone wrong and what decisions they've made out on the water are the wrong ones. All the decisions you make on the water during a tournament or a fun day of bass fishing will relate to your actions before you've gone fishing – tackle preparation, scouting before the tournament and learning what the bass are doing. By going through each of these steps, you'll prepare yourself to make right decisions on the water instead of wrong ones.

"Many times a fisherman will say, 'Well, I just guessed wrong,' but that's not really true. Maybe you haven't prepared yourself well enough to make a right decision instead of having to guess at one. I've learned that the better informed I am, and the more homework I've done, the better the decisions I make on the water. All the steps that have gone before my actually being on the water and fishing enable me to make better decisions

on the water when those decisions count. The more you know about the body of water you're fishing, your tackle and what the bass are doing, the more accurate the decisions will be that you make on lure choices and where and how to fish. Learning to make the right decisions on the water when they count is how you turn your bass fishing around from poor to great."

Secret #5 – The Best Game-Day Execution for a Bass Tournament

When we discussed Davis' fifth secret to being a better bass fisherman, he explained, "If you've done everything right up until this point, you have to be able to execute the fishing plan you've developed.

Execution is simply when you get a bite and put a bass in the boat: your line doesn't break; you don't make dumb decisions when you get the bass on the line; you don't miss bites; and you make the right cast, to the best structure, with the correct lure to get the bass to take your bait, so you can set the hook and put the bass in the boat. You have to execute properly and be sure when you cast your lure out that the bass will take the bait before the lure reaches the spot where the bass is holding. As soon as you set the hook, you have to start thinking: how you'll get the bass out of that cover now that you've got it on the line; and what you can do to get the bass through, over or around that cover without breaking it off the line or giving the bass enough slack, so it can spit or throw the lure. Now that the bass is coming to the boat, you have to decide the best way to land the bass – either lipping it or picking it up by its belly. You've organized your tackle, done your homework, learned what the bass are doing, found where the bass are holding and have the right lure, at the right time, in the right place to make the bass bite. Now, you have to put the bass in the boat and make those split-second decisions that will make you either lose or land the bass. This step is the easiest step where you can fall short.

"Too, you have to be able to forgive yourself. Sometimes when you're bass fishing, you'll lose the bass that may have caused you to win or perform better. The bass just beats you. You've done everything right, but the bass just gets away. The bass has shaken the hook, broken the line or torn-out the hook, because it didn't have the hook deep enough in its mouth. Something caused that bass to get away over which you've had no control. When you look back and say, 'There's not one thing I could've done differently in my execution process to have landed that bass,' you have to forget that bass and move-on to the next one. I don't care how good a fisherman you are, you'll lose some key bass that can make a huge difference in how well you perform. That's just the nature of the sport. If you don't forgive yourself quickly but instead brood over that lost bass, you can't continue to grow and become a better bass fisherman. That's what I've learned this year. These secrets have helped me perform better in 2010 and since then than I did in 2009, and I hope they help you, too."

Chapter 4 - Denny Brauer – the Babe Ruth of Bass Fishing

Editor's Note: Most people know that Babe Ruth was the Homerun King of Baseball, but they don't know that Babe Ruth also was the Strikeout

King of Baseball. We remember his victories but quickly have forgotten his defeats. Every time Babe Ruth struck out, he became more determined to hit a ball over the fence. Great athletes in every sport use defeat as a motivator for victory. Denny Brauer of Camdenton, Missouri, is in the top five of all-time money winners on the Bassmaster fishing circuit, and won the Bassmaster Classic in 1998. But at the 2010 Bassmaster Classic held on Lay Lake in Birmingham, Alabama, in February, 2010, Brauer totally struck out and didn't bring one bass to the weigh-in during the entire tournament. There are lessons to be learned about fishing and life not only from the victories, but also from the defeats. Since most of us strike-out in bass fishing more times than we hit homeruns, listen to Brauer, learn from him, and see how you, too, can take a fishing defeat and transform it into a fishing victory.

Fishing to Win

I asked Denny how you recover from a defeat like the 2010 Bassmaster Classic, and he explained, "I really don't understand the question. The Classic has ended, and it's behind me. In fishing, as well in life, you have to be willing to accept whatever happens. I had a game plan going into the Classic and told several media outlets that I didn't know whether I would win or finish last because my performance would depend on water levels in the lake, weather conditions and the bass' attitudes, all things I couldn't control. The bass were only moving-up to shallow water to feed a couple of hours in the day. I knew that if the bass were feeding, I could catch them. On the second day of the Classic, the bass never moved-up to feed, and on the last day of the Classic, I let two big ones get away. I don't regret anything I did in the 2010 Classic.

"When I go into a major tournament, I fish to win. Second place to me is as big a loss as last place. Anybody can go onto Lay Lake and catch a small limit of spotted bass. That's pretty easy to do. But what do you get out of that? You can save a little face and finish in the middle of the pack, which is what some anglers want. But that's not what I want. I want to win. If I'll be competing at the Classic, I'll be there to win. I owe my sponsors my best attempt to win – not to come in second or be in the middle of the pack, but to win. Most of my sponsors understand that if I don't catch bass, I just don't catch bass. But if I catch bass, I'll try to catch the bass that will win the tournament. That's the way I play the game. I use a loss like the 2010 Bassmaster Classic to motivate me to win."

Finding the Motivation to Win

Brauer mentioned that you use a loss, like not bringing any bass to the scales at the 2010 Bassmaster Classic, as a motivating tool to win. When I asked him how to do that, he replied, "Anytime a competitor has a bad tournament and doesn't finish in the place he thinks he should, that competitor isn't happy. I get really angry at myself when I have a poor performance in a tournament. Throughout my career as a fisherman, whenever I have a train wreck like the 2010 Bassmaster Classic, I really get highly motivated to win the next tournament. In bass fishing, there are a lot of variables, but they all fall into two categories – the variables you can control and the ones you can't. But you try to control as many elements as you can. When you don't perform well, you have to look at the factors that have caused you to perform poorly and decide if there's anything you may have done better. If there is, this knowledge should inspire you to make better decisions at the next tournament. But if the reason you've lost is because of a variable you can't control, then looking at that factor and realizing you've done the best you can is important.

"All a fisherman can do is to try to put himself in a position to win. If you do that and lose, you can say you've given it your best effort. In the sport of fishing, you have very-few opportunities to win, so learning to deal with a loss is very important. In every tournament, I feel I have something to prove. At times we hunt for reasons to get motivated, and the 2010 Bassmaster Classic was a pretty good hunt. I found a lot of reasons at the 2010 Classic to get motivated for the upcoming 2010 Bassmaster Elite Series."

Getting Organized and Ready to Win

When I asked Brauer what lures he'd depend on to turn defeat into victory, he told me, "The way the tournaments are set-up (the types of lakes and the places we'll be fishing), I have to use a wide variety of baits to win. I'll use the new Tour Grade Football Jig quite a bit in some of these tournaments. In the first two tournaments, I plan to spend a lot of time with Shadalicious. Many of the lures I plan to use will depend on the weather.

I like to flip, so the weather and the water conditions have to be right for me to be able to flip a tube, a jig or a creature bait. There are a couple of tournament sites where I definitely plan to use Pure Poison swim jigs. I'll be fishing a wide variety of lures, and the Rage soft-plastic lures will definitely play a major role in my tournament fishing in all the events.

"I'll pack my boat and my vehicle with all the lures I think I'll need. I want to be better prepared and organized for the Elite Series. Being organized and knowing where all your lures of every size and color are located is one of those variables you can control that will help you win."

Gathering the Best Information When You Fish

"I generally don't have any time to practice before the BASS tournaments I'll be fishing," Brauer reports. "I'll go from one event to the other, and I'm not sure if that's not better than spending time practicing. Each day you fish is a new day on the water, and you have to deal with the current conditions of that day. If you practice a lot before the tournament, you develop preconceived notions about where the bass are located, what they should be doing, and what baits they should be eating based on old information. The best information you can gather to let you know how and where to fish is information you'll learn when you reach the water and evaluate the conditions on that day."

Using an Eraser Helps Brauer Be a Winner

As Brauer and I talked further I asked him how his future plans related to his fishing and tournament preparation, and he replied, "Yesterday's gone. Today and tomorrow is all I can be concerned with because those are the days I'll have to perform. One of the best things a fisherman can do is erase the past, especially when he's had a bad tournament. Evaluate, and learn what you could and should have done. Or, if you've had a bad tournament because of the elements you can't control, then forget that tournament. You can learn and get motivated from bad tournaments, but you can't change the outcome. So, why worry about those outcomes? I try to find something good in every poor performance in a

tournament that will help me do better in the next one. That's the real secret of tournaments and life. When something happens that you can't change, then don't worry about it. Get over it, and use it to motivate yourself to be better next time.

"Every time I go to a tournament, I'll swing for the fence to attempt to win, especially in big tournaments. You have three opportunities to win in every season of bass fishing. You have an opportunity to win the Angler-of-the-Year title and a berth in the Classic, and when you reach the Classic, you have an opportunity to win the big show. In every Classic in which I've ever competed and every future Classic in which I hope to compete, I have but one goal – to win."

To learn more about fishing with Denny Brauer, visit www.brauerbass.com.

Chapter 5 - Kevin VanDam on 12 Months of Successful Bass Fishing

Editor's Note: Kevin VanDam tells us the five things that have made him so successful in tournament bass fishing, especially during the 12 months of 2010 and 2011 in which he won the Bassmasters Classic Championship and the Angler-of-the-Year title on the BASS circuit.

Prepare and Fish Your Strengths in Bass Fishing

VanDam said he thought the number-one reason he believed he was so successful in 2010 and 2011 was that, "I believe a lot of my success is due to my attention to detail, especially in my preparation before I fish. I'm very meticulous about my tackle. I want to make sure I have new line on my reels, and that all my lures have sharp hooks. When I know that my tackle

is the very best it can be and am assured that I can find any lure of any size or any color when I need it, then that fact gives me a lot of confidence. My preparation works for me, because I know how to prepare for me. I don't fish like Rick Clunn, Denny Brauer, Skeet Reese, Gerald Swindle or Greg Hackney. So, I prepare the tackle that I believe I'll be using in a tournament that will allow me to fish to my strengths each day. I prepare my tackle and my lures specifically to fit my style of fishing that I believe in the most.

"Then I try to find bass that I can catch, using the types of lures that I feel the most comfortable with on that day, on that lake. If you watch all the top professional fishermen on the circuit, you'll notice that they all prepare their lures and tackle to fish to their strengths. For instance, Denny Brauer can catch fish any way that he has to, however, I'm sure in his preparation, he spends the most time getting his flipping and pitching lures in his tackle ready to go, because those styles of fishing are his strengths. There's never just one pattern or one way to catch bass in any tournament. If you go to a tournament and listen to how the anglers are catching bass, each leader more than likely has used a different tactic to catch his bass. Therefore, in tackle preparation, readying and using the lures you have the most confidence to fish what you've determined are the strengths you have in bass fishing are critically important to your success. I try to make the technique that I have the most confidence in produce bass on any lake I'm fishing, but it doesn't always work out that way. But I've pretty much been able to do that."

Have Confidence in Being Successful When Bass Fishing

As VanDam explains, "Another key ingredient that I believe has made me as successful as I am on the water is confidence. I always believe that regardless of water, weather, wind conditions or the type of lake I'm fishing, I can catch bass. If we're fishing on a lake where I know everyone will be weighing-in a number of 4- and 5-pound bass like we will on Lake Guntersville in Alabama, I not only believe I can catch those size fish, I believe I can catch even bigger fish. Or, if we're fishing a lake where you're hoping and praying to get a handful of keeper bites, I feel like I can get those bites with my lures. Even if we have to check-in at the end of the day at 3 pm, if I don't have a good bag of fish at 2:45 pm, I still believe that in that last 10 minutes before I have to make a run to check in, I can catch the size and number of bass I need to win that day. I don't back-off during a day of competition. I don't slow down, and I won't accept defeat until all the fish are weighed in by the anglers. I think I was born with a competitive nature. I love to compete, I like to win, and I won't give up until a contest is totally over. I think Yogi Berra said it best, when he said, 'It ain't over, till it's over!'

"From when I first started entering bass-fishing tournaments when in my teens, I've always demonstrated that kind of confidence. However, in my early days of competitive bass fishing some anglers viewed me as a

cocky young kid. I don't think confidence is learned. I think a competitor is born with it - either you have it or you don't. I'm a come-from-behind fisherman. In many tournaments, I've had to come from behind to win. In the last two Angler-of-the-Year tournaments, I was pretty much out of the hunt on the first lake that I fished. But then on the second lake in both events, I came from behind to win. Every day that I fish, I try to learn how to be a better fisherman. And I continue to learn more and more each day. I learn how to figure-out patterns that produce bass quickly. Too, the more time I spend on the water, the faster I'm able to learn where the bass are, what type structure they're holding on, what water depth they're holding in, what type of lure presentation they will bite, and what color lure seems to be most important on that day. I spend probably 175 days on the water fishing per year and that's where much of my confidence comes from, because I've been tournament fishing for 20 years. I have a lot of experience to draw-from on how to fish under just about any weather or water conditions we may face. Also, because we've had tournaments all over the country on a wide variety of lakes, I now feel confident that I can go to any lake and find and catch bass. For instance, I can remind myself that back in 1998, I fished Lake Guntersville at about this same time of the year, under these same weather and water conditions, so possibly the same lures I caught the bass on then, will produce bass now. From those assumptions, I at least have a place to start trying to find and catch bass.

"Technology has probably been the biggest-single ingredient to change the way we all bass fish in recent years. The quality of depth finders we have now is far superior to the old flashers with which many of us started fishing. Humminbird's new Side Imaging Sonar has drastically changed the way I find cover and bass and the way I fish. Then when you add in the use of GPS receivers with mapping devices, we all have become better fishermen because of technology. And, I'm not the only one. Any angler can become more proficient and fish with far-more confidence with the new technology that we've seen in depth finders. I've learned that you need to embrace new technology as soon as you learn of it. When new and better ways to fish are introduced, I definitely want to learn about those new innovations. If you're going to fish the Bassmaster Elite Series, you better know about new innovations, new lures and new and better ways to fish. If you don't, you won't be competitive."

Use Your Body's Metabolism and Don't Be Afraid to Change

VanDam shares that another reason he's been as successful as he's been may be due to his body metabolism. "I don't know. Perhaps part of the reason I'm successful has to do with my body metabolism. I'm definitely not a couch potato. I don't like to sit around, and I don't like to loaf. And, one of my faults is that I'm not very patient. My style of fishing is run and gun. I cover a lot of water, I like fast-moving baits, and I like to produce a lot of casts in a day.

43

"However, there have definitely been some times in tournaments when after the tournament's over, I've realized I've fished too fast or left an area or a pattern too quickly. And the pattern or the area I've left may have been the place or the technique that will have won the tournament. However, I realize that hindsight is always 20/20. When I'm on the water, I believe that the best way for me to fish is to trust my instincts.

"At the Bassmasters Classic in February, 2010, I stayed in the same area for 3 days and didn't throttle-down and run from one end of the lake to the other. Finally, I think I have enough experience to know when to stay put as well as when to run and gun. Fifteen years ago, I wouldn't have fished 3 days in the same spot. Instead, my right hand would've been on the throttle, and my head would've been in the wind. Once again, I trusted my instincts. I felt I knew the size and the numbers of bass that particular spot could produce. And if I just stayed with that spot I had a chance to win. Now this was a big gamble for me. However, knowing the region as well as I did, I actually felt I was taking a low-risk gamble. I think I've put some bridles on Kevin VanDam that he hasn't had on him before. I've finally learned how to hold him instead of folding him. Like the lyrics of the song, 'The Gambler,' – 'You've gotta' know when to hold 'em, know when to fold 'em.'"

Rely on Your Instincts to Bass Fish Your Best

According to VanDam, "When I'm out fishing, and there's a weather or a water change or something in the environment is different than it has been, I have thoughts pop into my head like, 'Kevin, since the bass have moved more shallow, you need to put-up your Series 6XD and pick-up a Series 3 crankbait. Or, perhaps, instead of fishing ledges, you need to move to the visible grass.' Over the years, I've learned that when I'm not catching bass, I need to trust those ideas that pop into my head from out of nowhere. I think many people are afraid to take that kind of a chance, especially if they're fishing a pattern, a location or a bait that's been producing bass for them. You have to have a lot of confidence and belief in those ideas that seem to come from nowhere that tell you to give-up on a pattern that's not producing and try something totally different.

"But when you do that, you're doing what many of us call intuitive fishing. Yes, it's a gamble, and, no, it doesn't always pay-off. And, I think one of the things that helps anglers to become more intuitive fishermen is to not be afraid to fail. I know that by fishing intuitively, I'm still going to lose more times than I'll win. However, I also know if I'm fishing a particular area, type of bait or pattern, and I'm not catching bass, I'm not going to win staying with the technique I'm using right then. So, I'm willing to gamble on those thoughts that pop into my head from nowhere. I'll take that chance. Sometimes listening to that intuitive voice works out, but most of the time it doesn't. However, if you're not catching fish doing what you're doing, you really don't have anything to lose by learning to fish intuitively.

Probably 75% of the time an intuitive thought results in my catching more fish.

"And, let me tell you why. Even if I don't catch fish, when I follow my intuitive sense and make a change, whatever that change is usually leads me to a technique or a lure or a tactic that does produce bass. I've learned that my intuitive sense pays-off more often than it doesn't. I've learned that I can follow my instincts (intuitive thoughts), and that intuition generally will lead me to fishing better and catching more. And, I believe if as a fisherman you learn to develop and learn to rely on your intuition, you may find that it also works for you."

Don't Be Afraid to Fail

The last element that has enabled VanDam to have as much success as he's had is he's totally not afraid to fail. "I know that many people have great expectations for me. I do expect to win every tournament I enter. For instance, at the Bassmasters Classic, one of the worst fears that a tournament fisherman has to face at the Classic is walking across that stage without any fish in his bag. Your family's disappointed, your sponsors are disappointed, and you're disappointed. However, if that fear rules you, then winning the Classic becomes very difficult. Fear often will cause anglers to fish very conservatively, not take risks and not go after the win. In the Classic, most anglers want to make sure they have fish to show - whether they win or not.

"But I believe that to win a tournament, you've got to go into that tournament to win, not to just get points and not just to walk across the stage with fish in your sack. If you have that attitude of trying to win, then you're not afraid to take risks or go for broke to try and pull-off a win. An example of what I'm talking about is Denny Brauer and Greg Hackney, two of the best tournament pros I know. They both pull out all the stops and fish to win. Yet, Denny and Greg sometimes doesn't bring a single fish to the scales. When you have that kind of courage and are willing to roll the dice to win it all or lose it all, you'll lose more times then you'll win. But if you don't fish with that kind of reckless abandon, you'll never know what winning a tournament feels like.

"To fish with that kind of courage, you have to have experience, and you have to have tasted victory before. Sometimes when you make one of those gambles and that gamble pays off, you win. And winning is what many of us pros are all about. We've had that winning feeling before, and if we have to lose miserably to try and get it again, we'll take that gamble. This is one thing you'll see with all the pros. None of us fish for second place."

To learn more about Kevin VanDam and his fishing, go to www.kevinvandam.com.

Chapter 6 - Mark Rose – My Five Anytime and Anywhere Go-To Lures

Editor's Note: Mark Rose of Marion Arkansas, a professional bass fisherman, another more than $1-Million Winner and the 2007 FLW Series event winner, the 2009 Stren Series Championship winner on the FLW Circuit, the 2010 FLW Series event winner and the 2011 FLW Tour Major winner, takes chances and does whatever's required to win bass tournaments. This week, we'll take Rose to a mystery tournament at an unspecified lake in an unknown area somewhere in the U.S., with unidentified water and weather conditions, and he'll tell us his five anytime, anywhere, go-to lures.

Use His Survival Go-to Lure

Mark Rose and I were talking about lures, and when I asked him what the number-one lure he'd take with him to his mystery tournament was, he told me, "The first lure I'll choose is the shaky-head worm, consisting of a 1/8-ounce shaky head jig and a green-pumpkin-colored Super Finesse Worm. A shaky-head lure is like candy to a bass. The fish can't resist its subtle action. Also, the shaky-head worm is easy to see, sneak-up on and inhale. You can fish the shaky-head lure around any type of cover at any time of year, under any water or weather conditions, and it will catch bass all year. It can be fished around grass, tree tops, rocks, boat docks, riprap, and along bluffs. Too, it's appropriate for any water clarity. The shaky-head worm has helped me make a living as a tournament bass angler and take bass to the scales anywhere I've fished in the country. I rely heavily on it, and I'll always have one rigged on a rod in just about any tournament I fish.

"Also, the shaky-head worm is a good follow-up bait. If a bass misses your primary lure, many times you can pitch that shaky-head worm into the spot where the bass struck the original lure, and the bass will take the shaky-head worm. This jig-and-worm combination is my survival lure. The green-pumpkin-colored head and worm are the most-versatile of all the shaky-head jigs and worms, because they fit any water color, cloud cover or water condition. I fish the shaky-head worm on 8-pound-test line with a 6-foot 6-inch medium-action rod and a high-speed gear ratio reel. When I'm fishing in heavy cover, I may bump my line size up to 10-pound-test line. When you don't know what to fish, you're fishing a new lake and don't know how the weather conditions are affecting the bass, perhaps your bass are short-striking, or for some reason you aren't catching bass, then I suggest using the shaky-head worm."

Fish the Ocho Lure

I discussed with Rose what the number-two lure he'd put in his tackle box would be to fish this mystery tournament, and he commented, "A 5-inch Ocho in the Double Header color. This lure has green pumpkin on one side and watermelon red flake on the other. You can fish this color in any water color or condition. You can fish it deep, weightless, wacky style, in heavy brush, down a rocky bank, on a Carolina or a Texas rig, or with a shaky-head jig. My favorite way to fish this lure is with 15-pound-test fluorocarbon line with a No. 4/0 hook weightless, casting it to the edge of grass in open water or pitching it into cover. You can fish the Ocho around any type of cover you find. The Ocho is a subtle bait for when the bass don't want to bite, or if you don't know what the bass want to bite. You can rig the Ocho many-different ways and fish it on various types of cover or structure. I always can find a way to catch a bass on the Ocho.

"Also, not a lot of people fish with the Ocho. When you're going down a bank, you may say, 'That's a spinner-bait, a crankbait, a plastic-worm or a top-water bank.' Very rarely when you're surveying a lake do you look at the cover available and say, 'That's an ideal spot to fish the Ocho.' This lure doesn't come to mind readily, which is the reason I'm such a big fan of it. Most people don't think about using the Ocho unless they're desperate. So, it's the last lure in a tackle box most people will fish. Most anglers are power-bait fishermen – chunk and wind, get it, and go. So, you know all the bass on every lake have seen every chunk-and-wind

lure on the market. But more than likely, very-few bass have seen the subtle presentation of the Ocho, and that's what makes this lure so deadly effective for me."

Play with a Football at Any Time of Year

For Rose's number-three go-to lure in his tackle box for fishing this mystery lake, he explains that, "I've come to love the football head jig. When the bass are out deep on any type of rock cover, the football head jig is designed to come through that rocky cover where worm weights, Carolina rigs, other jigs and deep-diving crankbaits won't work as close to the bottom without getting stuck. Too, I like the football head jig because it's a big-bass bait. In a tournament, I'm not fishing for 1/2- to 1-pound bass. Rather, I'm trying to catch the biggest bass I can, and the football head jig is designed to catch big bass. I depend on the shaky-head worm and the Ocho to keep me from losing tournaments and getting embarrassed. I know I can put bass in the boat anywhere at anytime under any condition with those two lures.

"I also will look at what lure I should take to catch big bass and win the tournament, which is the reason I'll choose the football head jig as the third go-to lure in my tackle box. To jazz-up the bait a little, I'll put a green-pumpkin-colored Rage Craw on the back of a green-pumpkin-colored football head jig. I plan to fish this bait on 15-pound-test fluorocarbon line with a 7-foot medium-action rod. I'll drag the football head jig along the bottom, crawl it over every rock, drop it off every ledge and hop-it over every log. I use this bait when I fish off the bank on underwater cover."

Take the Red Eye Shad

The Red Eye Shad was the fourth lure that Rose selected to take with him to this mystery tournament. "The first two lures I mentioned, the shaky-head worm and the Ocho, are my always-catch-bass lures. I've also named the football head jig as my big-bass, deep-water lure. But I also need a search bait I can fish quickly, cover a lot of water with and still find and catch bass. That's the reason my fourth lure is the Red Eye Shad. I've weighed-in a lot of bass on the Red Eye Shad. The sexy shad has been the hottest color in the nation in the past few years, and it deserves that reputation. So, when fishing the Red Eye Shad, I prefer the chrome sexy shad color.

"The Red Eye Shad not only covers a lot of water and helps you locate bass, this bait also produces big bass. The Red Eye Shad is a good pre-spawn search bait and fall bait. If you have to fish it in the summer, you can fish it deep. I also use it like a depth finder. When I fish the Red Eye Shad on shallow flats, I can locate little patches of underwater grass in shallow water. I prefer to fish this lure on 15-pound-test line with a 7-foot medium-

action rod and a high-gear-ratio reel. You really need the ability to retrieve the Red Eye Shad fast to keep it off the bottom and out of the mud when you're fishing very-shallow flats."

Use the Old Reliable – a Spinner Bait

The last lure Rose picked for his tackle box to try to win this mystery-lake tournament was a spinner bait. "I can cover a lot of water with a spinner bait like I can with a Red Eye Shad. The spinner bait catches big bass like the football head jig, is as versatile as the Ocho and the shaky-head worm, and can be fished in and around any type of cover. If I only can take one spinner bait with me, I'll choose the 1/2-ounce Premier Pro-Model spinner bait with double-willowleaf blades and a chartreuse-and-white skirt. I almost can make a living as a professional bass fisherman with this one lure. I'll pick the Premier Pro-Model spinner bait, because on windy days when I can't fish the shaky head, the Ocho or the Red Eye Shad, that spinner bait is heavy enough that I can throw it into high winds and rough waters. You always can fish a spinner bait into the wind. Always anticipate these rough conditions, regardless of where you're fishing, and the time of year you're fishing.

"Remember, the wind is your friend when you're fishing a spinner bait. If you go to wind-blown banks and cover a lot of water with the spinner bait, you generally will find bass. You can run that spinner bait over grass or through lily pads, bounce it off rocks or cast it around brush piles, logs and blown-down trees. You can crash it into boat-dock pilings or yo-yo it along riprap. There's no place you'll fish where a spinner bait will be inappropriate. I prefer to fish the spinner bait on 20-pound-test fluorocarbon line. I like a 7-foot medium-heavy-action rod and a high-gear-ratio reel when I'm fishing a spinner bait.

"I'll choose the white-and-chartreuse-colored spinner bait, because I can fish this color successfully in extremely-clear or muddy water. I'll throw the shaky head and the Ocho when the water's really clear, but when the water's even a little stained, you need a lure with a lot of flash and color. That chartreuse-and-white color is very visible in lightly-stained or muddy water.

"I'd hate to go to a tournament with only five lures, but I have the best chance of winning any tournament at any time of year under any water or weather condition with these five lures. Even if you're fishing for fun, these five lures will help you solve almost any fishing problem, bring bass to the boat and enable you to have a great day of bass fishing."

To learn more about fishing with Mark Rose visit www.roseoutdoors.com.

Chapter 7 - How to Turn Your Bass Fishing Around to the Positive Side with Mark Davis

Editor's Note: Mark Davis won Bass Angler of the year in 1995, 1998 and 2001, and was the Bassmaster Classic Champion in 1995. But Mark had the worst year in 2009 of his fishing career. However, Mark returned to professional bass fishing with a vengeance. Mark made one of the biggest turnarounds in his professional fishing career that anyone has seen. All of us go through slumps. We all get down on ourselves about bass fishing. We've asked Mark Davis how he has come back from a lousy fishing season to having better fishing seasons.

A Little Bit of Difference

While talking with Davis about how he finished on the Bassmaster Elite Circuit in 2009, he explained, "I was down in 50th place somewhere. 2009 was the worst year in my entire fishing career. I decided I'd turn my fishing career around. Preparation has a lot to do with it. I believe the more time you spend getting ready to fish, the better you'll fish. Also, I've really been studying the lakes on the schedules, and then trying to go pre-fish them. Another advantage I've had is we've fished quite a few lakes where the bass have been in the post-spawn condition. That's normally a strong time of year for my style of fishing. I've also put in extra work effort, and I think all of these ingredients together have helped me this year. The post-spawn favors my style of fishing. After the spawn, the bass move out to deeper water and tend to gang-up and school-up. I've been able to catch a lot of bass on crankbaits like the Series 6 XD. I couldn't keep the bass off that lure at Guntersville. I easily could have caught 100 or more bass on the Series 6 XD each day I fished Guntersville. When we went to Clarks Hill, the bite was much-more difficult. The bass just didn't want to bite a crankbait for me, so I caught them on the Rage Lizard."

When we talked about what he was doing now that he hadn't been doing last year with his fishing, Davis stated, "Well, besides catching fish, I'm making better decisions on the water than I made last year, and I'm able to find fish and stay on them better than I did last year. At the level of bass fishing in the Elite Series now, there's a very-fine line between fishing in the middle of the pack and fishing at the head of the pack. I know a lot of people don't realize just how fine that line is. I think I've just been able to put the lures, the fish, my depth finders and the lakes together a little better

than I've been doing, and that little-bit better at this level of fishing can make a big difference in the size of the check you take home."

100 Bass a Day

In 2010, Davis had great success finding the bass and catching them, up to 100 bass a day, even culling some 5 pounders while fishing with the Series 6 XD. He explained to me that, "To start with, I got to fish Guntersville Lake in Alabama, which is a great fishery. It's always had

plenty of big bass – if you can find them. What made Guntersville good for mc and the Series 6 XD was the fish were spawning or had just spawned. Because so-many fish were spawning, most of the competitors fished for those fish, which took the pressure off the post-spawn fish out in deeper water. So, I was able to locate quite a few schools of post-spawn bass. These schools would be holding hundreds of bass on each spot I found, and I had identified 18 of these kinds of places before the tournament ever began. I was fishing river ledges. I'd crank the 6 XD down to 15 feet – even deeper on some spots – and run that 6 XD through those schools really fast. Once the school got fired-up and started feeding actively, I could catch one on almost every cast. Sometimes I'd even catch two bass at a time. I'd have one bass hooked on the front treble hook and a second bass hooked on the rear treble hook. Life and fishing doesn't get any better than that.

"I was fishing with the sexy-chartreuse-shad color. It has a blue-gray top with pale-chartreuse sides, and I've found this to be a really-great color to fish when the water has some stain to it. I was using 12-pound-test Stren line, making really-long casts and cranking the bait down on points and river ledges. Once I got the bait down, I'd reel it really hard and fast through the schools of bass. What I like about the 6 XD bait is that it can get down to those deeper depths without a fisherman having to stand on his head, put his rod in the water and almost have to crank upside down. I believe this bait was built for stand-up fishermen, not kneeling-down fishermen. The real secret to fishing the 6 XD successfully is to make long casts. Then you can get the lure down to the depths where the bass are holding, before you bring it through the school."

I was curious as to why Davis was retrieving the 6 XD so fast, and he explained, "I believe that during the post-spawn, the faster you can retrieve the 6 XD, the more excited the bass get, and the more eagerly they'll attack the lure. Some of those schools of bass that I found I believe you could catch a bass on every cast, while continuing to fish for 2-3 hours. I was using the All Star cranking rod with the Pflueger Patriarch reel with 12-pound test Stren line and cranking the bait really hard."

The Rage Lizard on Herring Lakes

Davis fished the Rage Lizard on Clarks Hill, and when he talked about how well he did while fishing there, Davis explained, "Clarks Hill is what we call a herring lake. The primary forage there for the bass is blueback herring, instead of shad, like you find on most of the lakes we fish. It's a very-challenging lake to fish, because the herring move-around quite a bit, and the bass tend to move with the herring. So, trying to keep-up with where the herring are can sometimes be a battle for a fisherman.

"To make the lake more challenging, when we arrived at Clarks Hill one year, the herring were holding in deep water, and the herring spawn was over. When the herring are spawning in shallow water, the bass fishing

is really good, and catching them is fairly easy. But once the spawn ends, the bass will go with the herring to those deep-water haunts. To make the situation even worse, the bass weren't very active.

"Most of the time I was fishing a 6-inch Rage Lizard in the green-pumpkin color on a Carolina rig to catch them. I dipped the Lizard's tail in chartreuse dye. Green pumpkin is such a good color on soft plastics just about anywhere you fish in the country. The fish at Clarks Hill bit that color really well. The Rage Lizard is a great lizard, because it not only has that Rage Tail on the end of the bait, but it also has the Rage action on the legs of the bait, making it a much-more active lizard than other plastic lizards. I felt like 6 inches was the perfect size for this lake, whether I was fishing the Texas-rigged lizard or the Carolina-rigged lizard. I had to fish really slowly and grind each fish out. I was fishing it in 5-12 feet of water, using a 3/4-ounce weight up the line, a barrel swivel below the line and a 4-foot leader with the end of the leader tied to a No. 2/0 hook. The leader length didn't really seem to matter. The real secret was to fish the Lizard really slowly. Most fishermen believe that the faster they fish, and the more water they cover, the more bass they'll catch. But sometimes fishing slowly can catch you a lot more fish than fishing fast will. What made this tournament even-more difficult was that we never continued to catch the bass on the same spots we'd caught them on previously. I never could fish the same spot on 2-consecutive days. I had to continuously be on the move.

"The bass were holding on main-lake humps on the bottom, just outside the spawning coves, which was exactly where you'd expect the bass to be holding after the post-spawn. They hadn't moved out to the really-deep water yet, but they were close to deep water. When I'm fishing a Carolina-rig like this, I don't get in a hurry. When I get a bite, I take-up the slack in the line and then use a sweeping hook set. Instead of jerking like you'll normally do when you set the hook on a bass, I just pull hard. Using this technique, you won't miss many bass."

The Importance of Going the Extra Mile in Your Bass Fishing

Davis did a remarkable about-face and was able to turn a bad year of bass fishing around and come back strong. Davis explained, "You have to remember, I've been competitively fishing for 25 years, and I've won a lot of big tournaments. Letting your guard down, getting a little complacent and slacking-off can be easy. You may not realize you're slacking-off, but that was the kind of season I had in 2009. When I look back on 2009, I say, 'Where did it all go wrong?' I know I went out every day and fished as hard as I could, even though I had a bummer of a season. Sometimes fishing as hard as you can isn't enough to consistently do well in bass fishing. Many times, you have to go the extra mile like a rookie does who wants to win a position on a professional football team. You have to be more prepared than the other fishermen by visiting the lakes ahead of time, so you can be familiar with the lakes. Then you have to work extremely hard in practice to know what the fish are doing, where they should be, and what they should bite."

You Need to Make the Best Decisions When Bassing

"At the end of the day, getting better at bass fishing comes down to making better decisions on the water when you're fishing," Davis emphasizes. "You may have more knowledge than any other fisherman on the lake, and you may work harder than any other fisherman in the tournament. However, if you don't make good decisions during the time the tournament is being conducted, you're not going to have a good season. I know this sounds simple and trite, but I've made better decisions on the water lately than I have in years past.

63

"You have to be thinking not only during the tournament, but before, after each day of fishing and the whole time you're involved in that tournament about what you'll do if fishing conditions change. Fishing conditions change daily and sometimes even hourly. You've got to be tuned-in to when those occasions occur and plan for how you'll adapt to changes in water color, cloud cover, wind, waves and many-other factors that are part of the fishing environment. When those changes occur, and you realize they have, you already know what you're going to do, since you've been thinking and planning for those changes. There are a lot of variables in fishing, and the people who win the most consistently are the ones who are aware of changing fishing conditions and have already planned how they'll adapt to those conditions throughout the day.

"A lot of this decision-making process comes with experience. Many times, the decision may be to throw-out everything you've been doing and every way you've thought you'll catch fish on this particular lake at this time and start all over again. You need to analyze the conditions, the type of cover you have to fish, the places where you'll find the fish and the way they're positioned on the structure or in the cover. You have to be willing to spend a day fishing in an area you've never fished before, because the conditions are right for that region. These ingredients are the ones that come together to allow you to make good decisions. I don't believe anyone can give you a 1-2-3 of here's what you should do list to make better decisions on the water. But there's one thing I can tell you that may help. Always remember that fishing conditions change throughout the day, and you have to be willing to make the decisions that need to be made to adapt your fishing to those changes.

"We need to remember that bass fishing is a sport. The only difference in our sport and other sports is we don't have a ball. However, many of the same factors that relate to football, baseball and basketball also relate to bass fishing. All of us understand the phrase 'in the zone.' When a basketball player is 'in the zone,' he can shoot from half-court and ring the basket. He's got confidence in what he's doing, he believes in his ability with the unknown, and he's got the courage to follow that inner voice that no-one else can hear. If a player 'in the zone' believes he can make a half-court shot, he'll make that shot. If a golfer believes that he can make a 30-yard putt, he'll make that putt.

"So, the first thing that has to happen to make right decisions on the water is you have to believe you can make right decisions on the water, even if your past history may suggest you can't. Whether you're a beginning angler, or you've been bass fishing for 25-30 years, making right decisions begins with your ability to believe you can, will and do make right decisions. The last couple of years I started out remembering the years that I had made right decisions and knowing that I had the ability to make those decisions back then. Somewhere deep inside me I knew I still had the ability to make right decisions on the water in the future. Confidence is the beginning point for making right decisions.

"Also, fishing is a game of momentum. Once you start catching fish and winning tournaments, you have every reason to believe you can continue to catch bass and do well in tournaments. So, momentum is another great ingredient to help a fishermen make correct decisions each day he's on the water."

Five Ways to Come Out of a Fishing Slump

After talking with Davis about how to make the best decisions on the water, and how he's turned his fishing around, I asked him to compare and contrast the differences in his season with Kevin VanDam's, and he responded, "Kevin and I are completely-different individuals, and we have completely-different philosophies of bass fishing. Personality-wise, Kevin is a go-getter. He's the epitome of a Type A personality. He uses that personality to fish very aggressively, cover a lot of water and catch a lot of fish. Kevin's also very attuned to fishing conditions and has proven that he can make right decisions on the water. Now I'm not nearly as aggressive on the water as Kevin is. I'm a slow-and-steady fisherman. I fish slower tactics than Kevin fishes, and I think that may be the best way to describe the differences in the two of us fishing.

"Now some years, where the bass tournaments are held and the mood of the bass on the lakes that we go to will lend themselves more toward one style of fishing than another style of fishing. The mood of the fish varies from lake to lake and state to state, and sometimes one style of fishing will produce better than the other. One year, fishing slowly and methodically has been the tactic the fish wanted more of than previously. Don't get me wrong. Both tactics will produce plenty of bass and win tournaments. However, some years, some styles of fishing just seem to produce better than other styles."

When discussing how to come out of a fishing slump, Davis names the five things that will help a fisherman.

1. Identify the tactics, techniques and baits that you believe you fish the best, and then go with what you're best at doing. As I've just mentioned, Kevin's a powerbait, fast fisherman, and he's won a lot of tournaments and been highly successful doing what he likes to do. I'm a slower fisherman, and I've been more successful fishing with slow fishing tactics than I have been with fast tactics. I'm not going to change and become a power fisherman. I'm going to fish the way I know how to fish to catch the bass on the baits I have the most confidence in and learn how to get better at the style of fishing that I like the best. Concentrate on the tactics and lures that you know help you catch bass.

2. Go back to the basics. Regardless of how good a football player you are, you've got to have the fundamentals of running, tackling, blocking and the other key fundamentals of the game to be successful. In my opinion, the fundamentals are:

    ◦ learn how to find bass: and

    ◦ keep your bass fishing simple, instead of making it so complicated, by you're learning to fish every new lure and new style that comes into our sport every day.

If you're fundamentally sound, with these two aspects of fishing, you can turn around your season. If you're not, go back to learning to read a depth finder, learning where you should look for bass at certain times of year and spending time on the various lakes doing nothing but trying to find bass. After you feel like you can locate bass on any lake, then learn how to catch them with the tactics you already know.

3. Keep all negative thoughts out of your mind. Negativity can slip into your mind like a thief in the night when you're not even paying attention, especially on a tough day of fishing. If you're having a hard day catching bass, you need to tell yourself, 'Okay, conditions are tough. The other fishermen are faced with the same conditions I am. I've got to make every cast and every bite count and produce a bass.' Many times, one or two bites will make the difference in winning or losing by catching a big bass. At the end of the day on difficult fishing days, making those one or two bites count can help your season be more successful.

4. Realize there's really no such thing as a slump in your bass fishing. We tell ourselves this to make an excuse for performing poorly. If you're not fishing well, if you believe you're in a slump, most of the time, the problem is between your ears, not out in the water. As human beings, we have the ability to choose to be happy or sad, to be positive or negative. You, not any one else, not any other circumstances, determine whether you're going to be positive and believe you're going to catch bass every time you wet a line; or negative, doubting that you'll catch a fish all day before you even put your boat in the water. If you've prepared properly, if you've worked as hard as you can, if you know you can and will make right decisions, and if you're tuned-in to the changing conditions in a day of fishing, and you know you're tuned-in, then you'll catch many-more bass than you will have caught if you tell your buddy when you get in the boat, 'I don't know what's wrong with me. I've been in a slump

for the last 6 months.' Well, brother, that kind of talk will keep you in a slump.

5. Learn to listen to your inner voice, and be confident that that inner voice is telling you the right things to do. Don't be out fishing during the day, make a decision on pure instinct, and 30-minutes later decide you've made a bad decision. One of the most-difficult aspects of fishing is to learn to follow your instincts (that inner voice) that are trying to guide you to success. Your brain is a computer. If you're constantly pushing buttons, rarely will it spit out the right data. But if you leave the computer alone and let it do its thing, it will give you the right answers more times than it will wrong answers.

A big part of following your instincts is not being swayed by the conversations you hear at the boat dock. For instance, as you're getting in your boat, you know you should be fishing points and ledges with a Carolina rig. But some guy who's just come off the water asks, 'How are you going to fish today?' and you tell him, 'I'm going to fish points and ledges with a Carolina rig.' He may say, 'Oh, no. You need to be fishing buzzbaits in the grass.' You've got to listen to your own voice and not the voices of others who probably don't know as much as you do. You'll do a much-better job of catching bass by following your own instincts than you will following somebody else's recommendations.

Now, just to make sure we're clear, don't turn-off your learning button. Learn all you can about bass fishing from everyone you can. But then when you get on the water, you're the only one responsible for how you perform that day, and you'll make better decisions than someone else who's trying to make decisions for you. Coming out of a slump is a head game. Learning to go from negative to positive is the way to turn the handle and start the door opening to get out of the slump. The other suggestions I've made will help you open the door wider, but you have to decide to walk through that door from being a loser to becoming a winner."

Chapter 8 - Professional Bass Fisherman Mark Davis' Five Career Turn-Around Baits

Thump Bass Fast

When Mark Davis named the five lures that helped him turn-around his bass-fishing career, he told me, "The Rage Thumper Worm's a 10-inch worm with a wide, sickle-type Rage tail and not a long ribbon tail like you'd find on the Anaconda. This Rage Thumper Worm is a great deep-water bait. I prefer to Texas-rig the worm and use a 1/2- or a 3/4-ounce slip sinker in front of it. Not many people fish with that heavy sinker in front of this worm; most anglers will use a 1/4- or a 3/8-ounce sinker. But if I'm fishing in 10-foot-deep or deeper water, especially when the water's hot, the heavier weight up front on that worm really works well. Too, I'll fish the Thumper Worm when the water's over 80 degrees, because that heavy weight enables the worm to fall really fast. Many times, particularly when I hop the worm off the bottom, the fast fall of the worm causes the bass to strike the bait, especially in hot weather. I've caught a number of big bass fishing that worm with a heavy weight."

Spin the Baby King Shad

The Baby King Shad was Davis' next lure of choice that helped him stay in the bass-fishing race. "When I first looked at the Baby King Shad, I said to myself, 'This is a great, natural-looking bait, and I'll catch plenty of bass with it.' And, that's exactly what I did – started catching bass. But new lures have secrets, and if you'll watch and listen to the lure, you'll learn secret ways to fish it that other anglers won't know. For instance, I've learned that I can put that Baby King Shad on a spinning rod, and fish it with 10-pound-test line. Now most anglers will fish the Baby King Shad on bait-casting rods. But a spinning rod allows me to cast the Baby King Shad much further than I can on a bait-casting rod. Too, a spinning rod enables me to cast this lure in high winds and gives me more control over my cast, than if I fished it with a bait-casting rod. I even can drop down to 8- to 10-pound-test line and retrieve the Baby King Shad really fast.

"Using this tactic, I can fish the Baby King Shad over submerged grass, around boat docks and on windy banks and points to trigger a number of bass strikes I can't get with other baits. One of my favorite places to fish the Baby King Shad is around boat docks. The spinning rod allows me to make accurate casts and deliver the bait to the spot where I think bass are holding."

Fish the Under-the-Radar Rage Smokin Rooster

Davis selects the Rage Smokin Rooster as another of his top-5 lures and says, "This lure has flown-under the radar of most bass fishermen.

When you look at it, you'll instantly think the Smokin Rooster is a flipping bait, and it's great for flipping heavy cover. But by watching the lure, I've learned that it's a dynamite lure to use on a Carolina rig, because it glides as it comes through-the-water. If you watch it carefully, you'll see its gliding action. Most fishermen won't look for another way to fish a lure like the Smokin Rooster, because when they see it, they tag it as a flipping bait. The Smokin Rooster has the Rage tail on the back and wings on either side. The lure is designed with a flap piece of plastic, so all the appendages of the bait have the Rage-tail action. I prefer to fish it with a 1-ounce weight and a 3-

or a 4-foot leader, just like I'll fish any-other Carolina-rigged soft-plastic lure. I've found this tactic to be especially effective during the spring.

"When I look at a new lure, I often say, 'That particular lure will be best fished this way.' Everyone else probably will look at the lure in the same way and come to the same conclusion. With the Smokin Rooster, I looked at the bait and determined that it would be a dynamite flipping bait, and then looked at it again to see how else I could fish the bait in a way no other angler probably would fish it. That's how I learned to fish the Smokin Rooster on a Carolina rig. Most of the time the bass will see the Smokin Rooster in a vertical presentation as it's flipped into or around grass, stumps or logs. The bass out on the points or on the ledges probably never will see a Smokin Rooster, especially behind a Carolina rig. So, even though there may be a number of people fishing a Smokin Rooster on the same day and on the same point I'm fishing, no one probably will be fishing it behind a Carolina rig. By using this bait in this way, I have an opportunity to catch the bass other anglers won't catch."

Shake the Rage Baby Craw for Bass

"The new Rage Baby Craw is another bait that has been productive for me," Davis reports. "We already had the Rage Craw, which is my

favorite all-around plastic lure to fish on a jig or a Texas rig. I looked at that little Rage Baby Craw and decided it would be a great jig trailer to put behind the Bitsy Bug when I wanted to downsize my lure and increase the number of bass I was catching. I'm sure that's what a lot of the other tournament fishermen were planning to do with the Rage Baby Craw.

"But as I began to look at that bait and watch its action, I decided to put it on a shaky-head jig. I prefer to rig the Baby Craw with a 3/16-ounce shaky-head jig and fish it on spinning tackle to give me a compact lure that looks like a baby crawfish in the water. Any bass that sees this bait will eat it. Another way I fish it is to Texas rig it with a small hook. I know how-many bass I can catch with a Texas-rigged Rage Craw. However, when the bite's tough, and the bass won't take that Rage Craw, I can downsize my lure and still fish a Rage Craw in a smaller, more-compact bait. When I rig it on the shaky-head jig, I can flip it in the grass, and it will look like a little hors d'oeuvre swimming right in front of the bass's mouth. A bass won't even have to move to take the lure. All it has to do is take a deep breath, and it will inhale that Rage Baby Craw. If you're fishing rocks using a Rage Baby Craw on a shaky head jig, you'll wear-out the bass.

"One of the most-successful ways I've used the Baby Craw is skipping it under a dock. When I'm skipping baits under a dock, most often I'll think of using a big bait out of which I can get a lot of skips. But by using the Rage Baby Craw and the shaky head jig, I can skip that bait to the far side of the dock in places I may not be able to get a bigger lure. I generally fish the Baby Craw with a shaky head jig on 8- to 10-pound-test

fluorocarbon line and a spinning rod. If I don't get any bites on my bigger baits, I'll try the Rage Baby Craw on a shaky head jig. Then I'll see the number of strikes I get each day dramatically increase. Again, the bait the bass see most often on a shaky-head jig is the worm. Nine times out of ten, when a lure's staying in one place and shaking, that lure probably will be some type of 4- to 7-inch finesse worm. But the bass haven't yet seen that Rage Tail Baby Craw standing-up and shaking. That's one of the reasons I can get so-many bites and catch so-many bass with it. If you're one bass short of a limit in a tournament, you can bet on this lure and tactic to finish-up your limit."

Bet on the Bottom Dweller for Bass

Last, but not least, in Davis' arsenal of five lures is the Bottom Dweller. "The 1-ounce Bottom Dweller will definitely be in my top-five arsenal. I've always loved to fish with a big spinner bait. I won the 1995 Bassmaster Classic slow-rolling a 1-ounce spinner bait. When I saw the new Bottom Dweller, I really got excited. It's a souped-up version of Strike King's old heavy spinner baits. But the Bottom Dweller has the right head design, which is critical to the effectiveness of a spinner bait. I've learned that I don't want a flat, shad-type head on a spinner bait that I'll be fishing deep. Those types of heads tend to cause the spinner bait to hang-up in heavy cover, like brush and stumps. The Bottom Dweller has a round head that will help the bait kick around brush and stumps on the bottom without getting hung-up.

"It also comes with the Perfect Skirt that can hide your trailer hook, and it has the new Raz-R-Blade High RPM blades that let you fish that spinner bait in deep water. I've fished the Bottom Dweller down to 25-feet deep and have caught a number of bass just crawling it along the bottom. When you first get most spinner baits, you have to tweak them in some way to make them perform the way you want. Having to tweak your spinner baits eats-up valuable fishing time, but with the new burner blades, this lure can be fished right out of the package.

"I like all the colors of spinner baits, but more times than not, I'll fish a chartreuse-and-white spinner bait. I really like the sexy-shad color, especially in clear-water situations. That sexy shad-colored Bottom Dweller is probably one of my favorite clear-water lures. If the water has some stain to it, like we find in most lakes, I'll probably use the chartreuse-and-white Bottom Dweller."

Chapter 9 - Things I Hate about Professional Bass Fishing with Denny Brauer

Editor's Note: One of the most-versatile and most-successful fisherman on the BASS circuit is Denny Brauer of Camdenton, Missouri, who has earned more than $3 million in tournament winnings from fishing Bassmaster and other tournament circuits, not including his endorsements and sponsors. Although he's tagged as a flipper and a pitcher, Brauer primarily fishes the jigging spoon, one of his favorite tactics, and also is deadly with the drop-shot. Too, Brauer is noted for his quick wit and his love of aggravating the press. When asked about the five ways he hates to fish, he smiled and said, "There's no way I don't like to fish. I love to fish every tactic and every lure, and I love every body of water where I tournament fish." When you see the twinkle in Brauer's eye and a smile as big as a Cheshire cat on his face after this type of statement, you instantly know he's hooked you again. He finishes with the words, "I have no negative thoughts at all about fishing." Then finally, with a big smile he says, "Okay, I'll throw you some bread crumbs." We can use Brauer's wisdom to become better bass fishermen.

Fishing Gin-Clear Water

As Denny Brauer says, "Many times on the Bassmaster circuit, we'll fish lakes where you can see down 20- or 30-feet deep. The main reason I hate that clear water is because I'm so limited in the number of techniques I can use to catch bass under these conditions. When we arrive at a lake this clear, such as Lake Mead in Nevada, I know I'll have to leave most of my favorite lures and tackle in my rod locker. To be competitive on these type lakes, I'll have to fish with tactics and lures I don't consider my strong suits. I'll have to put-down my flipping stick and baitcasting rod, pick-up a spinning rod with 6- to 8-pound-test line and downsize my lures to crappie-fishing-sized lures.

"Too, I don't like clear water, because I don't fish under these conditions enough to like to fish in that kind of water. I don't think downsized lures and finesse fishing will win many tournaments, except in extremely-clear lakes. There are so few lakes in the U.S. where you find water you can see 20- to 30-feet deep. If you study the sport of bass fishing, you won't see finesse fishing winning many tournaments. Finesse fishing may play a role in some tournaments and cause you to bring some bass to the scales, but rarely, if ever, will a tournament be won strictly on finesse fishing. Most tournaments are won by power fishing with jigs, spinner

baits and crankbaits. When I'm forced to finesse fish on one of those clear lakes, I feel like I've gone fishing, but not like I'm fishing to win, which is primarily my focus. I don't like fishing for second place or to try to get a check. When I enter a tournament, I plan to win."

Traveling Endlessly

Brauer and I discussed the boring road trips to the various lakes he fished, and he stated, "I hate the boring rides to and from the lakes we fish. There's a lot of beautiful country in the United States, but some of it becomes less beautiful after you've seen it 20 or 30 times. I really dread some of the drives we have to make to reach the tournament sites where we fish on the Bassmaster circuit. Many times fishermen from the East gripe and complain when we have to go to the California Delta to fish. But I love that drive. I've only been out there three or four times in my entire fishing career, and I like seeing that country. From Missouri to California, you see a lot of different scenery than you do when you travel in the East. So, I look forward to those drives. But when we have to go to the Potomac River along the mid-Atlantic Coast, and we have to drive through traffic in those big cities to reach where we'll be fishing, I absolutely hate it."

Not Being Able to Control Aspects of Fishing

According to Brauer, "If you look at bass fishing, you'll notice some of the best bass fishermen in the nation are perfectionists. They're sticklers for detail, dotting every 'i,' crossing every 't,' sharpening every hook, changing line daily and retying their lures after every catch. They'll know where every lure and tackle box is located in their boats. Although we're perfectionists, there still are certain things we can't control. I can't control:

- the weather. I can have the biggest school of bass found before a tournament and know I can catch those bass and win that tournament. But then the weather forecast turns 180 degrees from what has been predicted. I plan my strategy according to the weather and how it affects the bass. But when that weather makes a radical change, there's nothing I can do about it. If I'm fishing the back of a creek and catching good numbers of big bass, but then on tournament day a rainstorm blows in, and the back of the creek looks like a clay hole, with the wind coming from an unexpected direction, then that area with all those big bass probably won't be holding bass anymore.

- other anglers fishing a spot I've chosen to fish. Perhaps I've located a school of big bass in a place I'm sure no one else is fishing, because it's so far up a creek most bass boats can't reach it. However, if I'm in the second flight to leave the put-in, when I reach that spot, another tournament angler may be there catching those big bass I've thought no one else knows exist.

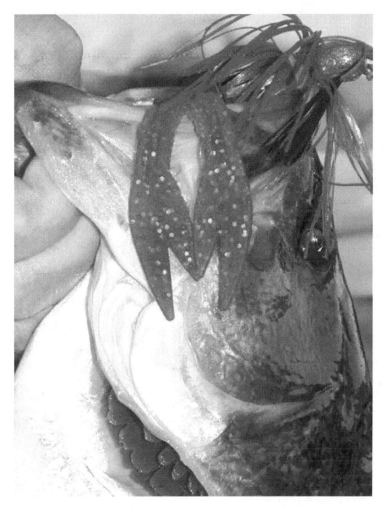

- bad things happening to my equipment. Although I maintain my boat, my electronics, my motor and every piece of equipment I depend on, for some reason, on tournament day, my engine may not crank. Problems will occur. I know they'll happen, and they happen every year. But I still get very aggravated when something I can't control interferes with my ability to find and catch bass and win a tournament."

Fishing in Bad Weather

Two other things Brauer told me while we were talking was he hated growing-up and bad weather, and he went on to explain it this way, "I grew-up bass fishing, and I used to love fishing in bad, nasty weather. The harder the rain blew, the colder the rain and the worse the weather, the more I loved it. My entire life I'd worked outside, regardless of the weather. So, when I started tournament bass fishing, I felt like bad weather gave me an advantage, because it narrowed the field of fishermen. I knew most of the competitors would be more concerned about why this bad weather was keeping them from catching bass, but I'd be thinking more about why this bad weather was helping me catch bass. I thought I had fewer competitors to fish against when we had terrible weather conditions, and I was right.

"But I've grown-up since then. My body isn't in the same shape it was when I thought I could eat alligators and spit out suitcases. The aches and the pains of a beat-up body don't fare well in rough water and cold rain. I've become a more fair-weather fisherman now. I really prefer hot weather and calm days – the type of day when a tourist wants to fish. I don't really like bad weather anymore, at least not nearly as much as did when I was younger. So, the last thing on my list of things I don't like about bass fishing is bad weather. Although we now have clothing and gear that makes bad weather far-more tolerable, I still have to say bad weather is something I really don't like."

Denny Brauer Realizes That What He Can't Control Can Have a Positive Side

Brauer hates when things out of his control interfere with his fishing. "I mentioned that I hate when events outside my control interfere with my fishing. I also told you that I know they'll happen. So, over the years, instead of staying upset throughout the day because the things I can't control have caused me not to win or to fish well in a tournament, I've learned to allow those aggravations to roll-over my back like water rolls over a duck's back. Over the years, I've taken a different approach. I try to fish as smart as I can and have as many-different game plans as I can to neutralize the negatives that will happen when I tournament fish. Like other competitors, I try to pay close attention to detail and prevent as many problems as I can before they happen.

"Too, in dealing with the negatives, I've learned that many times if not for the negative, I won't have done as well in the tournament as I have. I can remember a tournament on Chickamauga Lake in Tennessee

when I was in 10th place going into the last day of the tournament. All the contestants ahead of me were in the Who's Who of bass fishing - some of the strongest bass fishermen in the world. I knew the best I could do was a 10th-place finish against these great bass fishermen. On the last day of the tournament, I'd caught two little bass fishing a jig along a grass line. Then the wind came up and blew harder than the wind had blown all week. We had 4- to 5-foot-high waves out on the lake. This day was a classic example of one of those conditions I hated because I couldn't control the weather. Then I remembered that I'd graphed a ledge on the upper end of the lake that was loaded with baitfish, but I hadn't been able to get a bite on that ledge.

"My negative side quickly dismissed this thought with, 'That's a 30-mile run up the lake in 4- to 5-foot waves. There's no way you can make that run. And, if you do reach that spot without sinking the boat, you'll only have about an hour to fish before you have to make another long run to return to the weigh-in.' But my positive side said, 'Yes, but if the wind has pushed that bait up on that ledge, who knows, you may be able to catch one or two bass.' So, I went against reason, knowing that more than likely I would make the run and not catch any bass, and made the trip anyway. When I reached the ledge, I caught three giant bass and won the tournament.

"Therefore, even though I hate fishing when things I can't control don't allow me to fish where I want to fish, I've learned over the years that many times those terrible circumstances can cause me to fish in places I never will have fished and catch bass I never will have caught. Learning how to turn a negative into a positive oftentimes not only will save a tournament, but can cause you to win a tournament. Another factor I've learned over the years that most people run from and I have learned to run to is the willingness to lose. The only way you ever can win a bass-fishing tournament or catch a number of bass is to be willing to gamble on losing your chance to win."

To learn more about fishing with Denny Brauer visit www.brauerbass.com.

Chapter 10 - How Denny Brauer Picks the Lures He Fishes at Certain Times and Under Specific Conditions

Editor's Note: Denny Brauer of Camdenton, Missouri, one of the most-successful tournament bass fishermen in the world today, is known as one of the all-time best flippers on the Bassmaster circuit. "I flip because I want to fish spots most bass fishermen won't fish," Brauer says. "I fish to win every tournament I enter, and fishing thick cover with big baits gives me the greatest odds to catch big bass and win tournaments." But Brauer also flips tubes, creature baits and many-other types of lures to catch bass. To become a better flipper, we asked Brauer to tell us how he decides when and what lures to flip.

What to Flip and Pitch Every Season of the Year for Bass and Why

Denny Brauer grins as he says, "I have a new piece of equipment I've started using regularly that I can lower into the water and actually talk to the bass and let them tell me which lure they prefer on that day, on that lake, under that weather and water condition, when they're holding in a specific type of cover. I get a lot of feedback from the bass, and it only takes about 5 minutes. After I run through the program on this bass-talking device, I may discover that 80% of the bass say they prefer a jig that day. So, I tie a jig onto my line and start fishing. If you'd like to buy one of these bass-talking devices, I have a few more left to sell.

"Seriously, to make these types of decisions, the time of year and the water temperature are two of the primary factors that dictate my choosing jigs or soft-plastic lures. In the wintertime, in cold water, I've found over the years that the jig, the majority of the time, seems to be a better choice for flipping and pitching. There are certain things I do to a jig during cold weather to modify it. For instance, I'll take the Premier Pro-Model Jig and put a Denny Brauer Chunk on the back as a trailer, because this trailer doesn't have a lot of action.

"Once we get into the spawning season, I have to get a little more open-minded. When the temperature is 55 degrees and above, I look to the Flip-N-Tube, which is a compact bait without a lot of action. I prefer a green-pumpkin-colored Flip-N-Tube with chartreuse dye on the end of the tail, which resembles a bluegill when you put it into the water. Even though we don't always see the bass when we're flipping and pitching, the bass are setting-up around structure to start making their beds. That bait really triggers a lot of strikes for me.

"Then when the spawn has ended, I want a bait with more action. So, instead of flipping the tube, I'll start considering the Rage line of soft-plastic lures, like the Rage Craw, the Rage Space Monkey and the Rage Smokin' Rooster. When we get into the summer months, if I'm fishing a body of water that's not super-clear, I'll go back to the jig. But during the summer months, I want a lot of action from my jig. So, I'll put a Rage Chunk, or if I want a bigger profile, a Rage Craw, on the back of my jig, because these two trailers have much-more action than the Denny Brauer Chunk I've fished in the winter.

"Too, in the summer, I expect the bass bite to come on the fall. Those pincers that start flapping as the jig falls is like an invite for many bass to a crawfish dinner. Also, during the summer months, I'll fish the bigger-profile soft-plastic lures, like the Rage Hawg, which by the way is my number-one choice for summer and fall flipping and pitching when I think I need to be fishing a bigger bait. Or, if I think I need to flip a worm, I'll choose the Rage Anaconda or the Rage Thumper Worm. If I'm fishing clear water, I'll fish the Rage Anaconda. In stained water, I'll fish the Rage Thumper Worm, because it puts-out heavier vibrations than the Rage Anaconda does. During the fall, I go back to using creature baits. My number-one creature bait to flip and pitch in the fall is the Rage Hawg, and my number two is the Rage Space Monkey, at least until the water cools-down and drops-below 55 degrees. Then I'll go back to flipping and pitching the jig."

How to Choose Which Crankbaits to Fish

As we talked, I asked Brauer how he chose which crankbait he would fish on any given day, and he responded, "I use basically the same formula I do for picking flipping and pitching baits. There are warm-water crankbaits and cold-water crankbaits. One of the key factors that separate these two kinds of crankbaits is the amount of water each type of lure displaces. The other factor is the depth of water in which the bass are holding. This may surprise some people, but in the cold wintertime, my favorite crankbait is the Strike King Series 3. The Series 3 gives you a subtle presentation, and that lure is exactly the right size for catching wintertime bass. When you're dealing with cold water, many times you also will be dealing with clear water. So, when it comes to color, I'll pretty-much stay with the shad patterns of crankbaits. Once we get into the spring run-off when the lake starts to dirty-up, I'll choose the square-billed crankbaits, like the Series 1 and the Series 4S. The Series 4S is without a doubt my favorite early-spring crankbait. I beef-up the size of tackle on which I fish it. This bait has big hooks, so you can land bigger bass that may be holding in heavy cover when you fish the Series 4S.

"When bass get into their summertime mode, I prefer a Series 5 or Series 6 or the new Series 6XD crankbait. The Series 6XD is the most-awesome, deep-diving crankbait I've ever fished. When the fall rolls around, I'll go back to the Series 4S crankbait. I like that square-billed crankbait, and I prefer to fish it down the sides of logs lying in the water or around boat docks. Now, anytime you get advice like this, whoever's giving the advice is telling you how they'll fish, and how they choose lures in a certain section of the country. The patterns I've given you for flipping and pitching yesterday and for choosing crankbaits today are the lures I fish at

these times of year in the Midwest, since that's where I live. If I'm fishing
a lake with vegetation, instead of fishing the Series 3 in the wintertime, I'll
fish the Red Eye Shad. I'll also use the Red Eye Shad for fishing in the fall
when the bass are schooling on shad. Anytime you get this type of advice
from any fisherman, make sure you understand the types of lakes he fishes
and the choices he makes based on those kinds of lakes and the type of
cover found in those lakes. Bass fishing is much like selling shoes. Not all
shoes fit all feet at the same time and in the same way."

Why Denny Brauer Doesn't Like to Finesse Fish

"I don't fish the shaky-head worm very often, and shame on me for not fishing it more," Brauer reports. "The shaky-head worm is a productive way to catch bass, and the people who fish it and consistently fish it catch a number of bass. But my mentality says that when I have to start fishing finesse baits, like the shaky-head worm, crappie jigs, little-bitty crankbaits, tiny jigs and other smaller lures, I'm committing myself to not winning a tournament. It's easy for me to flip and pitch, but I'm just not comfortable fishing for small bass with little lures. Don't get me wrong. The shaky-head lure is deadly effective for catching bass, and that technique often will catch bass when nothing else works. But if you look back at the tournament records, very rarely will you ever see a tournament won using a shaky-head worm or any of the other finesse tactics.

"Here's the way I look at it. When I see a lot of tournaments being won by contestants with spinning rods in their hands and fishing shaky-head worm and other finesse tactics, then I may reevaluate what's required to win a tournament and get-out a spinning rod like other competitors. I'll start drop-shotting and fishing finesse worms and using all those little tactics. Right now, I don't see that happening, unless we go to a lake like Lake Erie. I fish to win, and finesse baits don't apply to my style of fishing or my fishing mentality.

"Remember that my style of fishing isn't the only way to catch bass or win tournaments. If that was true, I should win every tournament I fish. But each fisherman is different, and every fisherman has his own favorite style and philosophy of fishing. Just because I don't use certain lures or tactics doesn't mean those other lures and tactics aren't just as effective, and in some situations, more effective, than what I do. However, I believe in dancing with the date you've brought to the party, and flipping and pitching using big crankbaits, spinner baits and power fishing have enabled me to make a good living in the fishing business for many years. So, I don't think I'll change my attitude or my style of fishing."

How to Pick a Spinner Bait

"There are so-many spinner baits I can fish for bass that sometimes I get a little confused about which spinner bait to choose," Brauer comments. "So, I keep my spinner-bait choices fairly basic. I base my spinner-bait selection on water color, water temperature and the type of cover I'll be fishing, and how fast I want the spinner bait to run. Here are some suggestions for how to make effective spinner-bait selections.

91

1. The colder the water you're fishing, you probably will need to use a Colorado-blade combination on your spinner bait.

2. I'll choose either <u>Colorado blades or Indiana blades</u> in dirty water, because they'll disturb a little more water than a Raz-R-Blade or the willow-leaf blade will.

3. I prefer a Colorado willow-leaf blade combination, if I'm fishing a spinner bait slowly through the grass.

4. I'll use a gold-colored willow-leaf blade on the back of my spinner bait to give the bait some flash, if I'm fishing fairly-stained water.

5. I'll use a double willow-leaf-blade combination, if I want to move the spinner bait fast.

6. I'll fish a double willow-leaf-blade combination, because I can make those blades dance and do different motions that look like shad, if I'm seeing bass busting the surface and feeding on shad.

"After you determine which blades you need, then you have to start considering what weight of spinner bait you need to select. Spinner baits generally will run in water from 1- to 20-feet deep or more. That Bottom Dweller will get down deep and keep the blades turning, while you're fishing deep. So, here's the way I make my spinner-bait choices. When I open my spinner-bait box to choose the spinner bait I'll fish right now, the first thing I do is look at the water color, which will tell me the color skirt I should choose and the color and the type of blade I need. For instance, in dirty water, I'll have a white or a chartreuse skirt, and I'll probably lean more toward gold-colored blades. In clear water, I'll choose a more-translucent skirt and nickel-colored blades. Next, I look at the type of cover where I'll be fishing the spinner bait, which tells me the weight of the spinner bait I need. If you've got cold weather, you know you'll need a spinner bait that moves a little slowly, so you may choose a 3/8-ounce rather than a 1/2-ounce spinner bait. If you have warm weather, you may choose a 1/2-ounce spinner bait, so you can retrieve it faster.

"I think you need to set-up a specific tackle box as your spinner-bait box. You have to look at the spinner bait as tools for different fishing situations. And, you need to set-up your spinner-bait box to have various types of spinner baits in different colors, weights and blade combinations for any type of water, weather and cover situation you may fish. This way, you're not switching blades, skirts and sizes of spinner baits in the boat when the conditions change, or when you go to another lake. Most bass fishermen won't go fishing with only one crankbait or one size and color of plastic worm. You have to look at your spinner baits the same way as you think about soft-plastic lures and crankbaits. Remember, spinner baits are set-up for different types of fishing conditions, so have at least two or three for any type of fishing condition you may encounter."

How to Select a Big Worm to Fish for Bass

According to Brauer, the Rage Anaconda, a big fat worm with a lot of action, and the Rage Thumper worm may seem similar, but, "These two worms each give-off a different vibration pattern in the water. For instance, the Rage Anaconda is what I call a slither worm. It offers a big profile in the water, but it more or less slides through the water without giving-off a lot of pressure waves. This makes the Rage Anaconda a great clear-water worm and a deadly summertime worm. I live in Missouri, an area of the country that's ideal for fishing big worms. So, a 10-inch worm, like the Rage Anaconda or the Rage Thumper Worm, really appeals to me and a number of other Midwestern fishermen. I fish Truman Reservoir, as well as the Lake of the Ozarks, and that's where the Rage Anaconda really shines.

"To me, the Thumper Worm is a better dirty-water worm than the Anaconda. If I'm flipping tree tops in stained water, the vibrations produced by the Thumper Worm make it easier for the bass to find this worm in dirty water than they can the Anaconda. Also, if you're fishing a body of water that receives a lot of fishing pressure, any time you can offer the bass a bait they're not accustomed to seeing or haven't seen before, or that gives off pressure waves the bass haven't felt before, then use that worm. Because the Thumper Worm is fairly new, the bass-fishing waters in the United States have not been saturated with these worms. So, that gives anyone who uses a Thumper Worm an advantage.

"Too, most manufacturers make their lures, so that they only should be fished at a particular size. But the Thumper Worm is segmented, so if you want to use a Thumper Worm as an 8-inch worm instead of a 10-inch worm, you simply cut off the first 2 inches of that 10-inch worm. Then

you have a Thumper Worm that will perform just as well at 8 inches as it did at 10 inches. If you want a 5-inch flipping worm, that's one of the best flipping worms you can fish. Cut the Thumper Worm in half, and fish with the bottom end of the worm that has the goofy-looking tail. This worm was designed so that at whatever length you cut it, you still get the action the Thumper Worm has been designed to deliver.

"Both the Thumper Worm and the Anaconda are tools for fishing, and when I go fishing, I don't carry one of them and not the other. I take both styles of 10-inch worms. Even though you may think the place you're fishing is best suited for the Anaconda, because the water's clear and warm, the bass may decide they want the Thumper Worm that day instead of the Anaconda. I make sure I have any type of lure the bass may want to hit that day. Another reason for carrying two big worms is bass don't have big brains, but they are able to become educated. If you catch two or three bass out of a school of bass on the Anaconda, and the bass stop biting the Anaconda, then pitch the Thumper Worm to the bass. You're presenting a totally-different-looking worm with a different action. Many times you can get the bass to begin biting again and catch a few more bass in that school that may cause you to win a tournament. If I can take in my boat only two colors of plastic worms to fish with anytime and anywhere, I'll choose the green pumpkin and the plum."

To learn more about fishing with Denny Brauer, visit www.brauerbass.com.

Chapter 11 - Catching 100 Bass a Day with Roger Stegall

Editor's Note: The great baseball pitcher and radio announcer of days gone by, Dizzy Dean, once said, "It ain't bragging if you've done it." For 2-consecutive weeks in May, 2011, Roger Stegall, a guide on Pickwick Lake on the borders of Tennessee, Mississippi and Alabama, and an avid professional bass fisherman, averaged catching at least 100 bass a day with his clients.

Catch Bass Two at a Time

"At the end of May/first of June each year, the fishing is about as good as it's ever going to be at Pickwick Lake," Stegall reports. "My clients and I are averaging catching from 50-100 bass a day or more. We're catching a mixed bag of both largemouths and smallmouths. I believe the reason we're catching so-many fish at the end of May and the first of June is because high water and cool temperatures have increased the number of fish we're catching. We've had floodwater conditions five times this year at Pickwick

Lake. Now the water level is about stabilized, and the water is clear enough that the bass can see the baits. Too, the water temperature is making the bass feel very comfortable and aggressive, and the bass are really starting to school. We can fish two or three places at the most and catch 60-100 bass per day.

"The bass will be holding on secondary ledges and points – almost any type of structure that's off the bank that has a change in water depth. The bass seem to be holding from 5- to 13-feet deep. When my clients catch 60–100 bass in a day of fishing, they're very happy. One client recently had

on two bass on the same crankbait at the same time. One was a 3-pound largemouth, and the other was a 2-pound smallmouth. That same fellow from Virginia one day had two white bass on at the same time on the same lure, and then he had two largemouths on the same lure at the same time. Today, I had two largemouths on the same lure at the same time. In two days, we caught doubles on the same lure five times.

"The crankbaits we've been using and catching the bass with are a Series 5 XD and a Series 6 XD. The colors we're catching them on are pumpkinseed, sexy shad and chartreuse sexy shad. We're also catching them on the Premier Pro-Model double-willowleaf spinner bait with painted blades. The biggest largemouth we caught weighed 7 pounds. I caught the 7-pound largemouth and had another bass on that would have weighed close to 10 pounds. The biggest smallmouth we've caught weighed about 5 pounds."

Fish Series 5 XD and Series 6 XD for Post-Spawn Bass

According to Stegall, "I fish the Series 5 XD and Series 6 XD by casting upcurrent and cranking the baits down, until I hit bottom," Stegall explains. "Then I use a stop-start retrieve or a continuous retrieve. Every day, the bass seem to bite in a different way, so we have to change-up our retrieves to see which way they want the baits to come to them. Another lure I'll throw in late May is the football jig.

"However, with the crankbaits I use 10- and 12-pound Vicious Pro Elite Fluorocarbon line on a cranking rod with a cranking reel. I make a long cast upcurrent to try to cast past where the bass are holding. I fish a crankbait like I do a worm. When it hits the bottom, I stop it, let it float-up a little, crank it again, allow it to hit the bottom, stop it and then start it. I want it to work the bottom and float-off the bottom. Often, I'll pull the bait with the rod until it hits the bottom and then let it float-up and pull it again, until it once more hits the bottom. When the bass hit it, you don't have to guess whether you have a bite or not. Right now in early June at Pickwick, the bass are as aggressive as I've ever seen bass be. I'm seeing the fish with the depth finder before catching them. The bass are ganged-up, and they're pretty easy to find, if you know where to look.

"We're not having much competition for these fish and that's what's really strange. Right now, everyone is fishing up-against the bank, however, the bass are holding-out in that 5- to 13-foot-deep water. Most people have their boats sitting on top of the bass and are casting toward the bank, away from the fish. I think the bass are holding off the bank, because these are post-spawn bass, and their tails are red from fanning the beds. They've been setting-up on ambush points to feed on yellowtail shad. Three out of every four that we caught have shad in their mouths when we got them to the boat. I think these bass have just finished spawning and are pulling-out to these ambush points to feed-up heavily to regain their strength and body weights before they move-out to deeper water and their summer patterns. The people fishing the shallow water are fishing where the bass probably have been a week or two earlier in mid-May. Apparently, they haven't realized that the bass have pulled-off the banks and are holding on those first drop-offs away from the banks in a post-spawn pattern.

"Too, the type of bottom structure we're fishing doesn't seem to matter. We're fishing on clay bottoms, shell bottoms, rock bottoms and gravel bottoms. The most bass we've caught off one site during this time is 50-60 bass from one spot without ever moving the boat."

Spinner Bait Post-Spawn Bass and Move-Away from the Bank

In my conversations with Stegall, he mentioned that he caught some of his bigger bass on a spinner bait with painted blades, and went on to explain that, "I was fishing the Premier Pro-Model spinner bait with painted

blades in the chartreuse-sexy-shad, the sexy-shad and the silver-sexy-shad colors. These spinner baits had shad-colored blades with a dot on each of them. I was just casting the spinner bait out and slow-rolling it, and since the bass were eating those yellowtail shad, this spinner bait give me a yellowtail shad imitation, which was different from my crankbait. I'd cast the spinner bait out, let it fall slowly and then start a slow retrieve along the bottom. The bass would hit the spinner bait so hard they'd nearly knock the rod out of my hand. We were catching more largemouths than smallmouths, probably seven largemouths for every three smallmouths, with the spinner bait.

"I was fishing the 1/2-ounce spinner bait and if I was fishing a 10-foot bottom, I'd cast the spinner bait out, count it down to about 7 and then start slow-rolling it. Most of the places where I'd fish the spinner bait, I didn't have current. I'd be in the mouths of creeks or on secondary points

– anywhere I could find the bass ganged-up and feeding on shad. The bass were so aggressive that the current didn't seem to matter. They weren't always holding in or just off the current. Many times, they'd be pulled-back inside the mouth of a creek, holding on one of those bottom breaks where the shad were running. There's a huge population of largemouths in Pickwick, although Pickwick is primarily known for smallmouths. But the dominant bass are largemouths.

"I feel like I caught more fish on the crankbait than on the spinner bait, but I also know I caught the larger fish on the spinner bait. The size of bass that I was catching really seemed to pick-up when I started fishing the spinner bait. When my customers saw the bigger bass being caught on the spinner bait, they thought it was one of the greatest lures they'd ever fished. I think I can continue to catch bass like this into mid-June or so. Then the bass will move-out on the deeper ledges. They'll still be in big schools, but the schools will be further apart and a little more scattered.

"Most people don't think you can have good bass fishing right after the spawn. They think that after the spawn and before the fish move into their summer patterns that bass fishing isn't very good. But the reason they think that is that they've been catching bass in shallow water, and they continue to fish that shallow water after the bass have left. They don't realize that the bass have moved-out to the first or second bottom break away from the spawning area, and they're feeding-up on shad. The reason most people don't catch bass right after the spawn is they're still fishing the banks, and their boats are sitting on top of the fish they're trying to catch. You can have some of the best bass fishing of the year, if you follow those bass out after the spawn and look for them in that deeper water in about the same places they've been during the prespawn. The average size of bass we're catching right now is from 3 pounds up to 6 or 7 pounds."

Catch a Bass Easily on the Football Jig

Stegall likes the black-and-blue, candy-craw and green-pumpkin colors of football jigs in the 1/2- or 3/4-ounce size and matches the trailer to the color of the football jig. "I use the Rage Craw and the Rage Chunk in either green pumpkin or black," Stegall comments. "I just cast it out, let it go to the bottom and drag it on the bottom like I drag a weight on

Football?

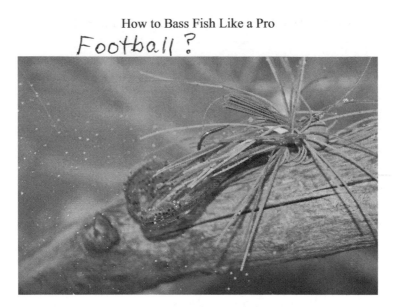

the Carolina rig. I start fishing the football jig when my arm gets tired of casting the spinner bait. When I'm fishing the football jig, I use a rod with a heavier action than I do with the spinner bait or crankbait. Using this setup, I can pick-up line quicker when I feel the bite and get ready to set the hook. I use 12-pound-test Vicious Elite fluorocarbon, when I'm fishing the football jig. What I like about fishing the football jig is when a bass hits that football jig, a 3-year-old child can catch the fish, because the bass sets the hook so hard that all you have to do is reel it in to the boat. What's so much fun about catching bass at this time of year on the football jig is that as soon as they feel those hooks on the bottom, they're coming to the sky.

"As far as catching more smallmouths on the football jig, the spinner baits or the crankbaits, we really can't separate the fish. The smallmouths and largemouths are schooling together, and the fish you catch are determined by which gets to the bait first. That's one of the fun things about fishing here at Pickwick Lake. When a fish takes a bait, you don't know whether you'll catch a smallmouth or a largemouth. Using the baits I've described, you don't know whether that fish will weigh 3 pounds or 7 pounds. They all school together in this post-spawn period.

"The Tennessee River, especially at Pickwick Lake, is such a great place for catching both largemouths and smallmouths, because the river is really fertile. Kentucky Lake all the way up to Fort Loudoun Lake on the Tennessee River are very-productive lakes to fish. But in the last 5-8 years, Pickwick has had an invasion of grass that has given the bass a place to hide, spawn and increase. The baby bass can get in that grass and hide from

the predator fish. We've had some tremendous spawns up here at Pickwick in the last 5 years, and we've got good populations of both shad and bream. There's plenty of bait for the bass to eat and ideal habitat for them to spawn in, raise their young and ambush bait. Pickwick is blossoming, I think that's due to the grass that's been introduced."

Fish Roger Stegall's Other Favorite June Lures

Roger Stegall wanted to try fishing something different at Pickwick Lake. He explained, "In June, I fished a finesse worm and caught a 5-pound smallmouth. Many times, there will be a big smallmouth in with a school of largemouths, so what I've started doing to target the smallmouth is use a shaky head in the 1/4- or 3/16-ounce size with either a green-pumpkin or green-pumpkin-red super finesse worm. I cast it out past where I've been catching bass and just hop it along the bottom. Those big smallmouths will often come in there and pick-up that worm, and you can catch them.

"Most people don't consider a finesse worm and a shaky head as a smallmouth bait for post-spawn smallmouths. But this lure will definitely catch those big smallmouths. I've found that most of the time, when I hop that King Shaky Head with a Super Finesse Worm on it, the smallmouths I catch will weigh between 3 to 5 pounds. People in many sections of the country consider a 3-pound smallmouth a really-big smallmouth. It's a

103

good-sized smallmouth, there's no doubt about it. But here on Pickwick, 5-pound smallmouths aren't that uncommon. We catch them fairly regularly, and there are days when we catch 6 pounders.

"The worm I'm fishing is 7-1/2-inches long. Different people fish the finesse worm in various ways. On the shaky head jig, you usually let it fall to the bottom, let it sit still for a few seconds, shake it, hop it, allow it to sit still, shake it and then hop it again. But I'm not shaking the worm at all. I'm just hopping it along the bottom. I'll hop it once or twice and let it sit still. Then that finesse worm will float-up and wave to the fish, until they come and eat it. A lot of times, when the bass quit hitting the crankbait, I'll switch to the Super Finesse Worm, and I can pick-up those bigger smallmouths. And, the Super Finesse Worm doesn't cull largemouths. You'll catch some largemouths on it too. But I've caught some really-good smallmouths on it, and I've got a lot of confidence in it.

"My customers are fishing the shaky head too. When they see me catch a bass, they generally want to fish with whatever I'm fishing. When we move to a new spot, they'll look at me and say, 'What bait are we going to tie-on now, Roger?' My job as a guide is to not only show my clients that there are bass on the places I take them to and help them catch the bass, but also to teach them to fish the lures and the ways I fish them. Then they can be successful on Pickwick and wherever else they go fishing.

"When the bass are really biting good is when you want to test new techniques and lures. So, when we got on a big school of bass up here, and we knew the fish were there, I rigged-up a Carolina-rigged Ocho in the green-pumpkin color. The Ocho has a little-different action than the shaky head does. The shaky head stands-up on the bottom, and the Ocho dives and darts. I caught some really-nice bass using that Ocho also. I use a dragging action like I do when I'm dragging a jig. One of the reasons I like to use the Ocho on a Carolina rig is because most people on Pickwick don't think of using an Ocho on a Carolina rig, but it can be deadly effective.

"I'm always experimenting with lures to see how-many different ways I can fish them. The best time to experiment is when you've got an actively-feeding school of bass. If you throw a lure into a school that's actively feeding, and you catch bass on it, then you build confidence in that lure and that tactic. But if you throw a lure all day long, and you never get it in a school of actively-feeding bass, you may think that lure won't catch bass. But the truth is, you probably never had that lure where there were bass. So, because we've been catching 50-100 bass a day, and I know where the schools of bass are and how they're holding, I can experiment with various techniques and lures to see if the bass will take them. If they do, that gives me a lot of confidence in that lure and in that tactic. That's the reason I tried the Ocho on a Carolina rig and found out that the bass would eat it up. We've had a great spring and early summer here at Pickwick. I've never seen better bass fishing, and I've never seen any lures catch more fish than the lures we've discussed."

To learn more about fishing with Roger Stegall, visit www.fishpickwick.com, or call 662-423-3869.

Chapter 12 - Mark Davis Explains How to Catch Hot-Weather Bass

Editor's Note: Mark Davis of Mount Ida, Arkansas, won the Bassmaster Classic and Angler of the Year in the same tournament season in 1995. Davis also won Angler of the Year in 1998 and 2001 and has participated in numerous Bassmaster Classics. More than just a professional angler, Davis is a nice guy, and here he shares with us how to catch bass in hot-weather conditions.

How to Catch Bass Now on Crankbaits

Although July and August are the hottest times of the year, Mark Davis says that using crankbaits produces bass then everywhere he fishes. "I'll be using the Pro Model 5XD, which is the right-size bait for this time of year. I prefer the medium profile in the summertime, because I can put it on 10-pound-test line and bump the bottom with it in 15 to 17 feet of water. That gives me a huge advantage in the summer. The colors of 5XD I've had the most success with at this time of the year are the citrus-shad and the sexy-shad colors. My favorite all-time shad color on a crankbait is Tennessee shad, which is a shad pattern with an olive-green back. That color is just hard to beat for catching bass in hot weather.

"When I fish the 5XD, I get the bait down and run it fast. In the summer, when the water gets hot, the faster you can run that crankbait, and the more excited you can get the bass, the more excited you'll get. At this time of the year, winding that crankbait fast is the key to getting those bass to bite. Now, you still need to have control over the crankbait and know what it's doing, and you'll still have to fish it over structure and cover. But speed is the key when you're fishing crankbaits in the hot summer. When a crankbait hits the cover, I give it a slight pause, stop my reel handle for a split-second and then start cranking again. The bass usually will take the bait when I pause-it or start-back cranking."

Why to Thump-Up Summertime Bass with Plastic Worms

According to Davis, his number-two bait for catching hot summertime bass is the plastic worm. "I prefer to fish the plastic worm in hot weather, and my favorite worm is the 10-inch Rage Thumper Worm. I'll fish this worm on 20-pound-test line and rig it Texas style with a No. 5/0 hook. Most times I'll be fishing it with a 1-ounce weight. When you're fishing 15- to 20-feet deep, you want a way to get the worm to the bottom quickly. The old way of worm fishing at this time of year uses the Bill Dance philosophy of, 'The lighter the weight you fish with, the better the fishing will be.' Now that's true most of the time, but when the water's hot, the same principle I've used with the crankbait for success is true with the

worm. The faster you fish it, the more bass you'll catch. A plastic worm that falls fast with a heavy weight in front of it will get more strikes when the water's hot than a worm that falls slowly, because the bass will give you a reaction strike rather than a feeding strike.

"Remember that when the water's hot, speed is the key to catching more bass. Sometimes you may need to use a 3/4-ounce weight in front of the worm to make the worm fall faster. I know a lot of fishermen who will say I'm crazy for putting a 3/4-ounce sinker in front of a plastic worm. But that same angler doesn't think anything about fishing a 3/4-ounce jig in 15- to 20-feet-deep water. If you're fishing a 3/4-ounce jig, why not put a 3/

4-ounce sinker in front of your worm? When the water's hot, many times a fast-falling worm will get more bites than a slow-falling worm will.

"Once the Rage Thumper Worm reaches the bottom, I'll just drag it on the bottom. Sometimes I'll swim the worm up and then let it fall back down. If I'm fishing in brush or grass, I'll fish the worm much slower on the bottom than I will on a rock bottom. During the summer months, you'll get a lot of bites on the initial fall. On some days, I'll throw the worm out, let it fall to the bottom, hop the worm three times off the bottom, allow it to fall back, reel-in the worm and then make another cast. You have to remember that at this time of the year, you're often fishing for suspended bass. So, the more times you cast-out your line and let it fall to the bottom, the more likely that you'll catch bass. Many times you'll cast-out the worm and let it fall to the bottom, and the first time you pick-up the bait off the bottom, you'll get a bite. When that happens, more than likely that bass has been suspended and has seen the worm fall through the water column where the bass is holding and has followed the worm on its descent to the bottom. So, the instant you move the worm, the bass will strike. My favorite, number-one color of the Rage Thumper Worm is plum, and blue fleck is my second-color choice. If the water's clear, I prefer the red bug color."

How to Use the Sexy Frog to Take Summertime Bass

"Another technique I use in hot weather is fishing top-water lures," Davis reports. "Top-water lures are always good in the summer, and the KVD Sexy Frog is really impressive. This bait's a great way to catch summertime bass with a top-water lure. I fish the frog on 65- to 80-pound-test braided line, and I fish it everywhere. A number of anglers think that the frog should only be fished around grass or lily pads. But that's not true. A frog is a top-water lure, just like any another top-water lure, and you can fish it in the same places where you'll fish a top-water lure. The KVD Sexy Frog is a good lure to fish in heavy cover, because it's weedless. I fish the frog on Lake Ouachita in Arkansas where there's no grass and catch bass. I'll catch bass on frogs on logs and any type of cover in the water. I'll also fish frogs around boat docks. Many times I'll fish the frog like a walking

bait, making the bait dart from side to side. Using this tactic, I'll catch a number of bass in open water.

"This KVD Sexy Frog is a little different from other frogs available in that it has a rattle in it, and it's virtually water-proof. Many of the frogs on the market will get water inside their bodies. When the frog gets water in it, you have to stop and squeeze your frog to get the water out before you start fishing again. This new frog has removable hooks and a tighter fit to prevent water from getting trapped inside the frog. I can make 20 or 30 casts, before I have to stop fishing to get the water out of the frog. Other frogs get water in them after only a few casts. Also, with this frog, you don't have to tinker with it. You just take it out of the package and start fishing.

"I fish three colors of KVD Sexy Frogs – white, black and a leopard-type color with a little white, a little yellow and a little black. When I'm fishing dark water, I'll fish the black KVD Sexy Frog. In clear water, I'll fish the white frog, and in stained water, I'll use the leopard color."

Why to Fish Buzzbaits for Hot-Weather Bass

Mark Davis explains that he catches a number of bass on a 3/8-ounce Tour Grade Buzzbait in hot weather. "This bait is ready to fish right out of the package. It has the perfect skirt that helps hide the trailer hook. I fish this buzzbait on braided line, and the new Tour Grade Trailer Hook helps me catch short-striking bass. I catch a number of bass fishing the buzzbait around stumps and lay-downs, as well as lily pads and any type of water vegetation. The buzzbait is much like the frog. You can fish it around open water, which very few fishermen do. I catch plenty of bass fishing the buzzbait over water, just like I catch a lot of bass on the frog in open water. If there's a lot of chop (wind) on the water, I'll catch bass fishing points using this buzzbait.

"I catch a number of bass on clean banks where a lot of fishermen don't fish, and there's not much cover. I think the number one-reason why I'm able to catch bass in places like this is because these banks are overlooked by other fishermen. These places don't look like they'll hold bass, so many fishermen will look at these banks and say, 'There's no bass there. I'm going to find a better-looking bank.' But there are some bass that do live on those banks, and if you'll put-in the time and fish the banks, you'll find features along the bottom that hold bass. Many times there will be key areas on those banks that hold numbers of bass."

Chapter 13 - Mark Rose Explains How to Catch Bass Now in Mid-Summer

Editor's Note: At this time of year, the most-consistent bass will be holding either on ledges or in extremely-shallow water. Mark Rose of Marion, Arkansas, has been a consistent fishermen on the FLW Tour Major Series Tournaments. Rose always is practicing to stay on top of his game and to develop new and better techniques for catching bass. Here's how Rose catches bass in mid-summer.

Keep-On Cranking with the KVD 1.5 and 2.5

Professional angler Mark Rose says he's become a big fan of the KVD 1.5 and 2.5. "I went on a fun-fishing trip on the White River in Arkansas, and we wore-out the spotted bass with those two lures. The KVD 1.5 and 2.5 are excellent shallow-water lures. You can tie either of these lures to the end of your line and cast it into any type of cover you see on the bank. I fish them under trees, boat docks and lay-downs. These two lures are virtually weedless. They work through the cover really well, yet still have a great action when you're fishing for open-water bass. I don't know all the reasons that bass like these two lures, and I don't have to know. All I need to know is that when I cast these lures out and reel them in, I catch bass. While fishing on the White River I used the sexy-blue-back herring and chartreuse with a black back colors.

"At this time of year, most of us don't think about bass holding in those 1- to 3-foot-depth zones. But, I fish the KVD 1.5 and 2.5 in the summertime in those shallow-water depths, because in the summer, generally the water's falling-out of the rivers and the lakes these river systems support. Then the bass pull into the cover. That's why I'll be fishing treetops and other bank cover.

"I use a steady retrieve and I don't try to slow-down the bait and walk it slowly through cover. I reel-in the 1.5 and the 2.5 immediately, because these lures are at their best when ricocheting-off cover. And, when they ricochet-off cover, that's usually when the strike happens. One of the big advantages of these two crankbaits is they're somewhat weedless. In the past, the two words weedless and crankbait never have been mentioned together. When you've tried to walk other crankbaits through cover, and they'll hit a limb, a stump, a rock or any other type of cover, then you've had to you'd stop your retrieve, let the bait float-up over the cover and then start cranking again. But with the KVD 1.5 and 2.5, you don't have

to stop your retrieve. You can just keep-on cranking when these baits hit cover, because they don't get hung-up very often. Using this tactic, I catch a number of 2-pound spotted bass and good numbers of 3- to 4-pound largemouth bass. One day when I was fishing with a buddy of mine, we probably caught and released 50-or-more bass with these two lures."

Catch the More-Aggressive Bass with the KVD 2.5

Rose said when asked, "You probably think, 'If I've got a KVD 1.5, why do I need a KVD 2.5?' Well, the KVD 2.5 gives you a bigger profile, and when the bass are more aggressive, they tend to hit the 2.5 a little better than they do the 1.5. Also, I use the 2.5 to catch bigger bass. On my trip to the White River in Arkansas, I knew I'd catch more bass in the 3-pound range than bass in the 3- to 5-pound-or-more range. I know from experience that the KVD 1.5 will catch more bass in the 3-pound-or-less range than bass in the 3-pound-or-more range. If I'm fishing with a number of 5-pound bass, I'll be fishing the KVD 2.5 more than the KVD 1.5.

"The 2.5 was designed to go about 1-foot deeper than the 1.5. But when I fish with the 2.5, I'm not fishing to pick-up that extra foot of depth. I'm fishing it more to have a bigger profile in that upper story of the water column. Another thing that I like about the 2.5 is that it has bigger hooks than the 1.5. We have No. 4 hooks on the 1.5 and No. 2 hooks on the 2.5. Those larger hooks make a big difference when you're fishing for bigger bass. On the Red River, I fished the 2.5 around stumps. Most people think that stumps sit in water where you usually can see them. But on the Red River, the stumps may be in 10 feet of water. I ran the 2.5 around the tops of those stumps. The bass were holding at about 4 to 5 feet, and the 2.5 was running at about 2.5 to 3 feet. The bass would come-up to tag that bait.

"When I'm fishing the 2.5 around cover, I'll be using 2-pound-test line, but when I'm fishing in open water, I prefer 20-pound-test line. When fishing the 2.5 around open water at this time of year, bass often will be concentrating on flag points and sandbars. On a river system, many times you'll find bass holding on sandbars, because there often will be natural springs coming-out on those sandbars. When you see a sandbar like this, the bass will be holding in really-shallow water. Some rookies need to have cover to fish the 2.5. In the summer and then later in the fall, the bass will be moving-around with big schools of baitfish. Later in the fall, the bass will be using schools of shad as cover. I normally use the KVD 2.5 to fish those schools of shad, but I'll also fish the 1.5, depending on the size of the bass normally produced by that river system. For 4- to 5-pound bass, I'll be fishing the 2.5. If I'm primarily catching 2- to 3-pound bass, I'll fish the 1.5."

Realize That Color Is the Key to Catching Bass in Hot Weather

While explaining that color is the key to catching bass now, Rose reports that, "I'm fishing a new color called the plum crazy. I've learned from the sexy-shad color that when you can find a color of lure that the bass really like, you can use that color for a number of different lures to increase the catch ratio of those lures. Most anglers know that plum is a great color for soft-plastic lures, especially on big plastic worms that are used in the

117

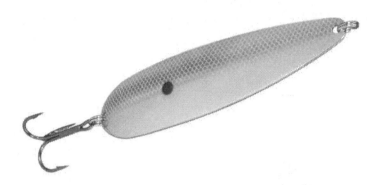

summertime. Now, the other color that's dominant in soft plastics and other lures is green pumpkin.

"In recent years, laminated-color lures have become more popular. If you look at crankbaits, the back of a crankbait is usually one color, and the side is another color. The same is true of a spinner bait. You may have one color on the head and a different-colored skirt, or if the head and the skirt are the same color, a different-colored trailer. The Bama bug color is a combination of June bug and green pumpkin with Okeechobee craw. The plum crazy color puts-together plum and green pumpkin. I've found that the bass really love this color, especially on the Tennessee River. I'll primarily be using the Rage Craw as a trailer in plum crazy, and I'll have a plum crazy skirt on my football head jig. I'm betting-on that combination. A number of fishermen on the Tennessee River fish ledges with jigs and soft plastics. I've learned that if I can show those bass a different color of these lures, oftentimes I'll get more strikes than if I fish the same colors as everyone else."

Recognize the Magic of the Sexy Spoon for Bass

One of Rose's favorite lures is the Sexy Spoon, and he explains that he's glad that most fishermen completely overlook this lure for summertime fishing. "The Sexy Spoon is a big, heavy lure, and many bass fishermen are intimidated by the size and the weight of that lure. They don't fish the Sexy Spoon, because they've never fished it, which gives me an advantage. When I'm fishing offshore, I have a lot of confidence in the 5.5-inch sexy-shad-colored Sexy Spoon. I prefer to fish it when the bass are holding in deep water, on ledges or on a rocky or a clay bottom with little or no wood. I like to see the bass feeding on shad. The secret to fishing the Sexy Spoon is to cast it out, let it hit the bottom, rip it off the bottom with your rod and let it fall back on the slack line. Then hang-on to the rod. The wobble and the flash of the Sexy Spoon is more than the bass can stand.

"When you make a long cast with the Sexy Spoon, you have a lot of line out. So, when you rip it up off the bottom, it won't really move very far. I just follow the line as it falls with my rod tip. I give the bed a big sweep and make sure I let the bait fall without any resistance to the line. I drop my rod tip and watch my line as it falls. The key to fishing a Sexy Spoon is slack line."

In deciding when to fish the Sexy Spoon and when to fish the football head jig in mid-summer, Rose explains, "I watch my graph. If the bass are holding tight to the bottom, I fish the Football Head Jig. If the bass are up-off the bottom in the middle-water column or feeding on shad on top of the water, I'll fish the Sexy Spoon. At this time of year, bass often will suspend, and that's when the Sexy Spoon really shows its stuff. When the bass are high in the water column chasing bait or up on top chasing bait, the Sexy Spoon is hard to beat in hot weather. Also, because of its weight and size, if you see bass schooling on the surface, you can cast that Sexy Spoon a long way and let it fall right through that school of feeding bass. I've fished the Sexy Spoon since it was introduced to the market. If you ever take that Sexy Spoon out and fish it on a good school of bass, you'll fall in love with it just like I did."

Understand When a Frog Is More Than a Frog

I wanted Rose's opinion on the Sexy Frog and when it should be fished, and he told me, "I really like the frog. I fish it sometimes not only in grass, but also in many-other types of cover. Most frogs steer-away from their hook by their line ties. When I saw how the KVD Sexy Frog was molded around the hook shaft, I knew then that this frog was unlike any other frog. I like all the colors for the Sexy Frog. Here's a big secret. Even

119

though it's a frog, you can use it with a bluegill color to imitate a bluegill when the bass are around the bluegill beds. You may be fishing on a dark day and want to skip that frog under banks but need a dark-profile bait. The black Sexy Frog in different shades and brown-colored Sexy Frogs imitate bluegills. So, I like all the colors, but the color I probably fish the most is black. However, I'll use all the colors for various types of fishing situations.

"There are many ways you can fish the frog. I catch a lot of bass at this time of year skipping the frog under boathouses, docks or in a brush top where I can't get any other lures. The KVD Sexy Frog is a top-water bait. When you put that frog into some type of cover where the bass never have seen a top-water lure, you drastically increase your odds of catching bass. When you place a frog in a treetop or under a tree where the bass are only accustomed to seeing a jig, a tube or a plastic worm, you'll get a strike where other fishermen don't. I prefer to fish it under a big boat dock that's low to the water in the hottest part of the summer, when oxygen levels are low in the lake, and the bass will move-up to the shade to stay cool and be closer to the surface of the water. When you cast that KVD Sexy Frog under a boat dock, there's a good chance that you'll catch a bass, because that bass never has seen a top-water lure come from that far back under a boathouse before. To catch that bass, all you have to do is rear-back with a 7-foot rod and skip that frog under that boathouse.

"I fish mostly braided line. The Sexy Frog is a fairly-large bait, so you need to get a strong and solid hook set when the bass takes it. That braided line allows you to really drive those hooks home. Another key to fishing the

Sexy Frog under boathouses and undercut banks is to fish it fast. I always try to work it fast, so the bass don't get a really-good look at the line. That's the reason I like 15-pound-test line when I'm fishing the KVD Sexy Frog. This size line is also good for skipping. When I'm skipping the Sexy Frog, I prefer to fish a 7-foot, 3-inch heavy-action custom-series rod that has a little tip action to help you skip the frog. Yet, it also has the backbone to drag those big bass out-of heavy cover or out-from under boat docks."

To learn more about fishing with Mark Rose visit www.roseoutdoors.com.

Chapter 14 - Catching Bass When the Weather Sizzles with James Niggemeyer

Editor's Note: James Niggemeyer of Van, Texas, guides fishermen on Lake Fork, fishes Bassmaster's Elite Tournament Series and also is a seminar speaker. Weather plays no role in whether or not Niggemeyer goes fishing. Water temperatures at Lake Forks often are in the 80s and 90s in the summertime with the air temperature at 90- to 100-plus degrees, and the heat index often more than 110 degrees. Here's how James Niggemeyer catches bass in these extremely-brutal conditions.

A Football Head Jig

James Niggemeyer finds bass when the air temperature is 100 degrees and more by fishing in 22-to 44-foot deep water. He explains, "I'm looking for bass that are chasing shad and eating yellow bass, and I'm using various lures to catch bass in 40 feet of water. The secret to catching those hot-weather bass is not to focus on one lure. One day we may catch fish on a football head jig with a Rage Craw Trailer, and the next day we may catch our bass on a KVD 5-inch Finesse Worm on a drop-shot rig. Or, later, the bass may want the Sexy Spoon, or they may take a football head jig in the morning and a Carolina rig in the afternoon. Or, they may want the 5XD or the 6XD. So, you have to fish a wide variety of lures to find out what lure the bass want on the day you're fishing, and at the time you're fishing.

"The first lure I'll be fishing in hot, dry weather, and what I'm catching most of my bass on is a 3/4-ounce Tour Grade Football Jig in the green-pumpkin color or the peanut-butter-and-jelly color, my two go-to-colors. On the green-pumpkin Football Jig, I use a green-pumpkin Rage Craw Trailer, either Summer Craw, or I'll fish the amber Bama craw for a trailer on the peanut-butter-and-jelly-colored Football Jig. I'll have my boat sitting in 30 feet of water and will cast toward the shallow side of the structure. In different spots, I'm fishing in 22 to 44 feet of water, and I'll fish with14- and 16-pound test-line. When Lake Fork has had drought conditions, and the water's really clear, I'll use SunlineShooter Fluorocarbon line. My rod is a St. Croix Legend Xtreme in a 7-foot medium-heavy rod, and I'm using an Ardent XS 1000 Baitcast Reel."

When I asked Niggemeyer to explain his retrieve with a football head jig, he answered, "The first key to catching hot-weather bass on the football head jig is to make sure the jig falls vertically on a slack line. If you engage your reel when the bait hits the water, the jig will fall like a pendulum, causing the jig to swing-away from the spot to which you're casting the bait. When you're fishing in deep water, and engage the reel when the jig hits the water, the jig will hit the bottom 5- to 6-feet away from the place to which you're casting it. I'm casting the jig to shallow water and fishing it back through the deep water. This way I can cover all the depth zones where the bass may be holding.

"On some days, the bass may be holding a little shallower than they do other days, or they may be holding deeper. Many days I'll just drag the football head jig like I do a Carolina rig. On the days when the bass are super-aggressive, they'll often take the jig on the fall. Other days, I'll rip the football head jig off the bottom and let the football head jig fall. Then the bass will take the bait on the fall. If the bass hits the jig as it's coming-up in the water, when you try to reel-down to the bait, you'll have a hard time making contact with the lure. If the bass picks-up the jig and is swimming toward you as you're taking-up slack, you may see the line go to the left or to the right and at the same time, keep contact with your bait.

"When you get a bite while you're dragging the football head jig on the bottom, sometimes you'll feel a hard thump on the line from a bass, and on other days you may only feel a slight peck, like a bluegill trying to take the bait. When this happens, lift-up on your rod, and your line will feel somewhat heavy and spongy. In deep water, sometimes the bass will take the bait very aggressively, and on other days they don't."

The Sexy Spoon

"The Sexy Spoon is fun to fish, and I like to fish the 5-1/2-inch Sexy Spoon in the green-gizzard-shad color," Niggemeyer recommends. "I also like to use the gold/black color. I cast the spoon out and let it go to the bottom. Then I rip it off the bottom with a hard upper sweep of my arm. When I sweep my rod, I'm probably moving 5 to 6 feet of line and causing that Sexy Spoon to move-off the bottom. As the spoon begins to fall, I watch my line. Once I see the line move to the left or the right or jump, I set the hook. Sometimes you won't see that you've got a bite, but as you start to sweep the rod up, you'll set the hook on a bass. Fishing the Sexy Spoon is a really-exciting way to catch bass. I've also noticed that the Sexy Spoon catches a better quality of bass than some of the other lures do. That big Sexy Spoon has become one of my favorite ways to catch bass. I've also caught some white bass on the spoon, but we don't have any saltwater stripers or hybrid striped bass in Lake Fork. I've had as-many-as three or four bites before on the Sexy Spoon after one cast.

"I use 20-pound-test-fluorocarbon line when fishing with the Sexy Spoon, because the 5-1/2-inch Sexy Spoon is a heavy lure, I can make long casts with it. When you make long casts and rip the bait up-off the bottom several times before you get it to the boat, you're putting a lot of stress on your knot. That 20-pound-test line slows-down the fall of the spoon more than if I'm fishing it on 14-pound-test line. As the bait falls, it flutters, causing the bass to bite the bait. I use a 7-foot 6-inch rod called the Pitching Rod. This rod is longer than the rod I use to fish the football head jig on, but I want the longer rod to sweep the line up to cause the spoon to come-off the bottom. I want the power in the rod. Then if the bass takes the spoon at

the end of the cast, while the spoon's falling, I've got enough power in the rod to get a good hook set.

"I think more fishermen aren't fishing the Sexy Spoon in hot weather, because many bass fishermen are somewhat intimidated by a 5-1/2-inch lure, which is probably why they're also not fishing the big Shadalicious swim bait. They look at those two big lures and say, 'How big has a bass got to be to eat a lure that big?' They don't realize you can catch a 10-pound bass on a 5-1/2-inch lure. I've nicknamed the Sexy Spoon the 'Car Fender,' because it's a big, really-heavy chunk of metal. It's different from any-other lure we use in bass fishing. The lure weighs 1-1/4-ounces. Fishing two

126

baits this heavy takes some getting use to, but once you get on a bite from deep-water bass during these hot summer months, you'll find out just how addictive this lure can be. Another reason this lure is so effective is because there's not many people fishing it.

"Something else I like about the Sexy Spoon is that it stays in the bass's strike zone longer than a crankbait. Even when I rip the spoon up 5- or 6-feet off the bottom, I'm not moving it very far from the spot where it's been before I've lifted it up. You may have to make five or six casts with a crankbait to get the type of reaction strike you can get with one cast of the Sexy Spoon."

The Game Hawg

According to Niggemeyer, "Another lure I've been using when fishing for these hot-weather, deep-water bass that's been very effective is the Game Hawg on the Carolina rig. The Game Hawg is smaller creature bait than a Rage Hawg, and the bass seem to really like the action of this soft-plastic lure. I cast the Game Hawg out on a Carolina rig and let it sink to the bottom. I've got a 3/4-ounce sinker up the line and a plastic bead above the sinker. Next I tie-on a No. 7 swivel and then 16-pound-test Sunline Shooter Fluorocarbon line onto the bottom eye of my swivel. I'll attach an XPoint No. 3/0 offset Round-Bend Hook and attach either a watermelon-green-and-red Game Hawg or a pumpkin-colored Game Hawg. Once the weight reaches the bottom, I drag the weight slowly through the water. The real key to catching the bass on this type of lure is to drag the bait and then let it sit absolutely still on the bottom. That Game Hawg sits still on the bottom, right in front of the bass's nose, and is so easy for the bass to inhale, that the bass just can't leave the bait alone.

"I let the Game Hawg sit still on the bottom for maybe 10 seconds before dragging it again. Bass in hot weather have a high metabolism, therefore they're more willing to feed than they are if the water's cold. But just because their metabolism is high doesn't mean that they're willing to chase baits over a long distance. When fishing in hot weather, you either have to drop the bait in-front of their faces and get reaction strikes, or you have to let the bait sit still, close to the bass. Then they don't have to expend much energy to get the bait. When you're fishing in hot water like the weather we have in Texas, you have to fish like you're fishing in really-cold weather and give the bass plenty of time to see and take the bait."

Finesse Worms

James Niggemeyer enjoys fishing for summertime bass with the Perfect Plastic Finesse Worm and rigs it two-different ways. "I use the KVD Perfect Plastic Finesse Worm on a Texas rig and on a Carolina rig," Niggemeyer says. "The colors I like best are the A-Magic and the blue fleck. I like the blue fleck on the Texas Rig. I like the A-Magic

on the Carolina rig. The A-Magic has three different colors- a greenish back, a blue vein and then a sandy-brown-colored bottom. I'm fishing the KVD Finesse Worm on the same type of Carolina rig on which I fish the Game Hawg. Sometimes the bass want a slow, do-nothing, subtle type of presentation. The Game Hawg has legs and appendages that kick, flutter and wiggle, and some days it's a really-deadly lure to use on the Carolina rig for bass. On other days, bass don't want to see a lot of action, and that's when I'm using the 6-inch KVD Finesse Worm.

"I fish the Finesse Worm around structure, around some brush piles and some what I call rough areas. When you're dragging a heavy weight, like a Carolina rig or a football jig, you may feel that weight go-over a rough spot that's rocks or just an irregular region along the bottom. Or, you may feel a lot of debris along the bottom. The bottom of Lake Fork where I primarily fish has plenty of standing timber, stumps and laid-down logs. When I'm dragging a Carolina-rigged worm on a sandy bottom or a rough bottom, I don't really slow the bait down very much. However, when I go over rocks, logs, limbs or debris, I really slow the bait down and give the bass time to come-out of their cover. When I rig Texas style, I fish the KVD Finesse Worm on 16-pound-test Sunline Shooter Fluorocarbon, with a 3/8-ounce bullet weight up the line and a 4-ounce hook. I'm dragging the bait slowly and shaking it a little bit with the rod tip."

Crankbaits

Niggemeyer prefers fishing the Series 5XD and the Series 6XD crankbaits in hot weather for bass. "These two crankbaits perform well when you're fishing offshore structure at this time of the year. My favorite color is the sexy-shad, but if the water's stained, I prefer the blue-powder back over chartreuse. But day-in and day-out, sexy-shad has proven to be the most-productive color when I'm fishing crankbaits. I make the longest cast I can, so I can get the lure down to the bottom and bounce it off the cover. To get that long cast, I'm using 12-pound-test Sunline Shooter Fluorocarbon line, and I'm casting the lure on a 7-foot 4-inch bass crankbait rod.

"Sometimes the bass will be suspended, and they'll take the crankbait before it gets-down to the bottom. And, often a school of bass will push a ball of baitfish to the surface and start feeding on them. That's one of the reasons I keep a crankbait tied on my casting rod on my front deck at all times. These two crankbaits will catch schooling bass, when you see the bass feeding on the surface. Another lure that will catch schooling bass is the Sexy Spoon, so it's always on my casting deck too.

"When my crankbait hits the structure or the bottom, I'll try a variety of retrieves. I'll stop the bait after it hits the structure, reel it three or four turns on the reel and stop it again for a stop-and-go retrieve. Sometimes

when the crankbait hits the structure, I'll speed-up the retrieve, and at other times I'll slow-down my retrieve. I vary my retrieves and let the bass tell me which retrieve they like the best. During the 100-degree weather in July last year, we were catching 25 to 40 bass a day with 2-1/2 to 3-1/2 pounders common and 4-6 pounders not unusual. Recently, we caught a bass that weighed 8.3 pounds.

"Another tactic that's paying-off for me right now is the drop-shot tactic. I've been fishing the KVD 5-inch Finesse Worm in either candy-craw, watermelon-red or double-header colors. I'm using 7-pound-test Sunline Cyber Fluorocarbon line with a 1/4-ounce drop-shot weight and a size No. 1 XPoint hook, about 10-inches up the line from the weight. I cast the drop-shot rig out and slowly drag it across the bottom, and sometimes I'll shake the rod tip. The drop-shot rig can really be effective when you've been fishing a school of bass, and they quit biting. Using the drop-shot rig, we can usually get a few extra bass, and often some of the biggest bass we will catch all day long will be caught on the drop-shot rig."

To learn more about fishing with James Niggemeyer, visit www.jamesniggemeyer.com.

Chapter 15 - Hot-Water Bass Tactics with Denny Brauer

Editor's Note: Denny Brauer of Camdenton, Missouri, one of the most-successful professional bass fishermen, depends on the tremendous database he keeps in his head that he's acquired from bass fishing for many years to win bass tournaments. Here Brauer will tell us how to catch hot-water bass.

Why Fish for Bass at Night in Hot Weather and Water Conditions

When Denny Brauer was asked how to find and catch bass under hot-weather conditions, when temperatures reach over 100-degrees Fahrenheit in the South, with a heat index of 110 to 115 degrees, he responded, "Hot weather is no longer just a southern phenomenon. Missouri and much of the Midwest also are experiencing 100-degree-plus temperatures. All the landscape where I live is a nice shade of brown right now. We've had 100-degree-plus temperatures with about a 115-heat index for over 8 days.

133

Under that type of extreme heat, very-few anglers want to go out on the water to fish, because catching bass in 90-degree water is difficult.

"But anglers won't give-up fishing; they'll just change the hours when they fish. Most bass fishermen right now are fishing at night. The best baits for nighttime fishing in hot weather are spinner baits, the Rage Thumper Worm and buzzbaits in darker colors. You'll get more bites and catch more bass fishing at night in this very-hot weather. If the body of water you're fishing has a thermocline in it, search for places where the thermocline comes into contact with a key piece of structure, like a point, a ledge or an underwater treetop. These structures can be found at 20- to 30-feet deep. At night, the bass move up to more-shallow water to feed, so catching them is easy. In the daytime, bass concentrate under boat docks where they find shade from the heat and plenty of bluegills, one of the bass's favorite baits at this time of the year. I also like to fish boat docks in hot weather, since they have some type of brush underneath them.

"To find and catch bass at this time of the year, look for areas on the body of water that you fish that can breathe (receives influxes of aerated water), such as creeks running into a main lake, eddy currents, drain-offs where water drains into a lake or windy points. Fish those areas rather than moving into pockets or coves that don't have any moving water. Bass want to be comfortable, just like you do. So, shade and cool-water runoffs are very important to them. Look for shade, higher-oxygen content and cooler water.

"I won the 1998 Bassmaster Classic at High Rock Lake in North Carolina fishing in the middle of the day in 2-foot-deep water. There was more oxygen in that 2 feet of water than in any-other parts of the lake. The bait was holding in that shallow water, and the bass were concentrating there, feeding on the bait. Most bass fishermen overlook boat waves. I won that tournament on the main part of the lake, where there was a lot of boat action and a lot of waves hitting the bank. We know that wind blowing into a point oxygenates the water, thereby causing the bass to bite. But we forget boats make a wave action that crashes against the bank, oxygenates the water and causes a feeding frenzy on the shad, which makes the bass bite. So, waves from water skiers and other boats oxygenate the water, causing bass to feed in shallow water, even in the middle of the day."

How the Tour Grade Night Spinner Bait Produces Bass in the Dark

Brauer mentioned to me that he fished the spinner bait at night to catch bass in the summer and explained, "I prefer to fish the new 1/2-ounce Tour Grade Night Spinner Bait. I use the single-blade spinner bait exclusively for night fishing. I use 20-pound-test line with this spinner bait, and I mainly fish it on points. I like the black-and-blue spinner bait with the black blades, but I also have done well with the black spinner bait with the gold blades. However, the black spinner bait with the black blades gives a darker silhouette. There's a new color called Tequila Moonshine that I like. This purple-colored bait is a productive color for night fishing. I cast-out

the spinner bait, let it flutter to the bottom and reel it slowly. I also fish it in brush piles at night.

"I don't use a trailer on my spinner bait when fishing it at night, because the Tour Grade Spinner Bait has the Perfect Skirt, so you don't really need to use a trailer. While I'm night fishing, I very seldom use a trailer, but when I'm fishing the spinner bait in the daytime, I'll use a trailer hook most of the time. At night, I let the spinner bait fall all the way to the bottom, jump it off the bottom, and let it fall back and/or fish it down through the cover. I don't really think I need the trailer hook. I usually like 15- or 20-pound-test line, depending on how deep I'll be fishing and at which depth the bass are holding. Fishing a spinner bait at night is a much-cooler way to find and catch bass than getting out in that hot afternoon sun."

Why to Fish the Rage Thumper Worm at Night

Brauer discusses another lure he uses to catch bass at night – the Rage Thumper Worm. "There are two really-big and productive worms – the Rage Anaconda, which came out a few years ago, and the Rage Thumper Worm. The Rage Anaconda doesn't have as many vibrations as the Rage Thumper Worm does. At night, the bass hone-in on the vibrations much more than they do in the daytime. So, I'll use a worm that displaces a lot of water and moves, like the Rage Thumper Worm. Even if the water's clear,

I still prefer the Rage Thumper Worm. But instead of the 10-inch worm, I may use the 7-inch worm. In clear water, I like to fish a 10-inch worm, because I prefer to catch big bass rather than numbers of bass. I also like the 10-inch Rage Thumper Worm, because it's a segmented worm. So, I can cut-off as many segments as I want to make that worm any length I want it to be.

"Also, the tail on the Rage Thumper Worm displaces a lot of water. Most of the strikes you'll get on the Rage Thumper Worm, even at night, will occur when the worm is falling. When you're fishing at night, any of the darker-colored worms will be productive. I wish there was a black-colored Rage Thumper Worm for night fishing, but there isn't, so I fish with June bug, a dark color. I catch a lot of bass on it at night. Blue fleck is another productive color for night fishing. California craw is a pretty-good

color, but to successfully catch bass on a plastic worm at night, use darker-colored baits."

How to Fish Jigs for Bass at Night

Brauer enjoys fishing jigs around boathouses at night. "I like to fish the Pro-Model Jig around boathouses at night. I like the 1/2-ounce jig instead of a lighter jig, because I want the jig to catch a keeper-size bass. I usually put a chunk behind the jig. I fish the black-blue-colored jig on 20-pound-test line. I especially like to fish the jig around the boat docks with brush under them. This is a great way to catch a big bass at night. When fishing the jig at night, I make a long pitch of the jig to the back of the boat dock, let the jig fall straight to the bottom and then crawl it over the bottom, until I get the jig into the brush. Then I use the jig to bump the brush. I've found that summertime bass want to hang-around brush piles more than any-other type of structure. A number of prey and predator fish will use a brush pile underneath a boat dock as cover. So, when you let that jig sit in the brush pile, don't be in a hurry to get the jig out of the brush pile. Remember, most times bass aren't aggressive in the summer. If you let the jig sit in the brush pile and just start tapping it against the limb (especially as I get higher-up in the brush pile), you'll be surprised at how-many big bass you can get mad using this technique.

"I primarily crawl the jig to stay in contact with the bottom, until I get it in the brush pile, and then I'll start working the jig through the brush pile. I'll hop the jig if I'm fishing it out on points at night. Also, the jig can be extremely deadly on points, especially on the main lake at night. When I'm working the jig down a point, I generally hop it rather than drag it. Don't hop the jig if you come to a brush pile on that point, because you'll get hung-up. Just drag it up the limbs until you reach the top limbs, shake it, and then let it fall back into the brush."

Why to Fish the Buzzbait around Bank Structure at Night

Another lure Brauer uses at night to catch bass occasionally is to fish a buzzbait like the black Pro-Model Buzzbait down banks. "I especially like banks with 45-degree angles. I also prefer to fish the buzzbait on points. I really like to fish the buzzbait during the transition times, such as that last hour after dark and the last hour before daylight. Those are key times to fish any top-water bait throughout the summer months. If you're going to fish that buzzbait around structure, you have to find out what type of structure is in the lake you'll be fishing, such as blown-down trees or logs around the bank, bushes bordering the water or grass in the water. That's where you'll need to be fishing. The bass will be holding in the area where you find that bank structure.

"Remember, if you've got clear water (which often happens in late summer), bass will be holding in deeper water and won't stray far away from it. So, the ends of bluffs and boat docks with deep water and big water underneath them are where the bass will move to feed. Search for shallow-water areas where the bass can move from deep to shallow water quickly, feed and then get back to that deep water. You have to know the depth of the lake you're fishing. In some lakes, deep may be 5 feet, and shallow may be 1 foot. In other lakes, 100 feet may be deep, and 5 feet may be shallow.

"I prefer to fish a steady retrieve, and I don't fish it fast. I want the bass to be able to hone-in on that buzzbait. I usually fish the black Tour Grade Buzzbait with a trailer hook. Oftentimes when fishing a buzzbait at night, you'll hear the strike rather than see it. So, I set the hook on the buzzbait just like I do when I'm fishing a plastic frog. I hesitate just a moment before I set the hook. That's the reason I prefer a slow retrieve. With a slower retrieve, your reaction time will be a little slower than if you use a fast retrieve. By using a slow retrieve, a bass will be able to inhale the bait when the fish attacks it. Also, the slow retrieve means you're less likely to pull the buzzbait out of the bass's mouth."

To learn more about fishing with Denny Brauer, visit www.brauerbass.com.

Chapter 16 - Bassmaster's 100 Best Bass Lakes

The editors of *Bassmaster* magazine released the results of the first annual 100 Best Bass Fishing Lakes in the U.S. Falcon Lake in Texas took home the top prize, followed by Lake Okeechobee in Florida.

The list was compiled through a months-long process reviewing research from state fisheries agencies, nominations from B.A.S.S. Federation Nation tournament organizers and a panel of widely traveled professional anglers, fishing writers and others.

Magazine 2012 100 Best Bass Lakes in the U.S.

Falcon Lake, Texas

1. Falcon Lake, Texas

2. Lake Okeechobee, Florida

3. Lake Guntersville, Alabama

4. Lake Erie, Michigan/Ohio/New York/Pennsylvania

5. Lake Champlain, New York/Vermont

6. Lake Amistad, Texas

7. Lake Minnetonka, Minnesota

8. San Joaquin Delta, California

9. Lake Coeur d'Alene, Idaho

10. Clear Lake, California

11. Rainy Lake, Minnesota

12. Pickwick Lake, Alabama/Mississippi/Tennessee

13. Lake St. Clair, Michigan

14. Oneida Lake, New York

15. Toledo Bend, Texas/Louisiana

16. Kentucky Lake/Barkley Lake, Kentucky/Tennessee

17. Grand Lake, Oklahoma

18. Kezar Lake, Maine

19. Sam Rayburn Reservoir, Texas

20. Columbia River, Washington/Oregon

21. Kissimmee Chain Of Lakes, Florida

22. Candlewood Lake, Connecticut

23. Santee Cooper lakes, South Carolina

24. Roosevelt Lake, Arizona

25. Lake Winnebago, Wisconsin

26. Lake Fork, Texas

27. Louisiana Delta, Louisiana

28. Lake Ouachita, Arkansas

29. Lake Konawa, Oklahoma

30. Lake Of The Ozarks, Missouri

31. Potomac River, Maryland/Virginia

32. Shasta Lake, California

33. Lake Havasu, Arizona

Lake Okeechobee, Florida

34. Lake Michigan, Wisconsin/Illinois/Indiana/Michigan

35. Mille Lacs Lake, Minnesota

36. Florida Everglades, Florida

37. Lake Charlevoix, Michigan

38. Lake Mead, Nevada

39. Choke Canyon Lake, Texas

40. Lake Seminole, Georgia/Florida

41. Congamond Lakes, Massachusetts

42. Table Rock Lake, Missouri

43. Lake Winnipesaukee, New Hampshire

44. Falls Lake, North Carolina

45. Umpqua River, Oregon

46. Okoboji Lake, Iowa

47. Red River, Louisiana

48. Pueblo Reservoir, Colorado

49. DeGray Lake, Arkansas

50. Trap Pond, Delaware

51. Bull Shoals Lake, Arkansas/Missouri

52. Spirit Lake, Iowa

53. St. Lawrence River, New York

54. Squam Lake, New Hampshire

55. High Rock Lake, North Carolina

56. Arbuckle Lake, Oklahoma

57. Lake Tarpon, Florida

58. Apache Lake, Arizona

59. Lake Powell, Utah/Arizona

60. Perry Reservoir, Kansas

61. Chickamauga Lake, Tennessee

62. Lake Wawasee, Indiana

63. Smith Mountain Lake, Virginia

64. Lake Conroe, Texas

65. Noxon Rapids, Montana

66. Diamond Valley Lake, California

Lake Guntersville, Alabama

67. Summit Reservoir, Nebraska

68. Lake Hopatcong, New Jersey

69. Rend Lake, Illinois

70. Lake Pleasant, Arizona

71. Lake Audubon, North Dakota

72. Flaming Gorge Reservoir, Wyoming

73. Harris Chain Of Lakes, Florida

74. Cobbosseecontee Lake, Maine

75. Ute Lake, New Mexico

76. Susquehanna River, Pennsylvania

77. Wilson Reservoir, Kansas

78. Elephant Butte Lake, New Mexico

79. Lake Oahe, South Dakota

80. Gull Lake, Minnesota

81. Kerr Reservoir/Buggs Island, N.C./Virginia

82. Dale Hollow Lake, Tennessee/Kentucky

83. Lake Gaston, North Carolina

84. Bullards Bar Reservoir, California

85. Dworshak Reservoir, Idaho

86. Tygart Lake, West Virginia

87. Keith Sebelius Reservoir, Kansas

88. O.H. Ivie, Texas

89. Lake Wallenpaupack, Pennsylvania

90. Lake Murray, South Carolina

91. Lake Sammamish, Washington

92. Lake Eufaula, Alabama/Georgia

93. Enid Reservoir, Mississippi

94. Old Hickory Lake, Tennessee

95. Fort Peck Reservoir, Montana

96. Manasquan Reservoir, New Jersey

97. Lake Mohave, Nevada

98. Lake Lanier, Georgia

99. Sebago Lake, Maine

100. McPhee Lake, Colorado

How to Bass Fish Like a Pro Q&A: A Conversation with Author John E. Phillips

Question: John, how did you get all those interviews and photos with the fishermen in this book?

Phillips: I've known most of these men since they started bass fishing. From the inception of tournament bass fishing, I've been going to national professional fishing tournaments, meeting and interviewing the pros, and on many occasions I've fished in the same boats with them at Bassmaster Classics and sponsored tournaments all over the country. The men in this book are friends of mine who work and play in the same profession that I do, and are willing to share their knowledge with me.

Question: John, why do you write about other fishermen and not write stories about how you fish, and why you fish the way you do?

Phillips: That's a question I'm often asked, and to answer it, you have to understand my philosophy about my writing career. When I was a very-young writer, I talked with some of the greatest fishing writers of the day, and one told me, "John, look at all the outdoor writers that are at this writers' convention. They fall into two categories: The ones who want to be heroes, and the ones who want to write about heroes. Over the years, if you'll watch, the ones who want to be the heroes usually have much-shorter careers than the writers who choose to find the heroes and write about them." I took that advice to heart and have been following that writing style for most of my life. But there's a second reason I write about the heroes instead of trying to be a national professional fisherman. I want to learn how to become the best fisherman I can be, and to do that, I realize I have to learn from the best fishermen who ever have lived during my lifetime.

Question: John, how long have you been a bass fisherman?

Phillips: The first fish I ever can remember catching was when I was 2-years old, sitting in my daddy's lap on a dock, holding a cane pole. My older brother, Archie, had caught a bream and put it in a bucket. When I wasn't looking, he swam under the dock and hooked the bream on my line. I not only caught that bream, but I was hooked on fishing for the rest of my life. Growing up, the two things I was the most excited about and looked forward to more than anything else were going fishing and hunting with my dad and brother. I can't remember a time when bass fishing didn't play a major role in my life. When I went to college, I took a squirrel dog that I kept in the closet of my dormitory room, an 18-foot aluminum boat, and an 18-horsepower Johnson outboard motor. I hunted and fished at least 4 days a week, not only for recreation but also for food for me, my wife and some of the other students in the married students' apartments.

Question: John, don't you believe that bass fishing is a constantly-changing sport, and you have to always be changing your tactics and lures to continue to catch fish?

Phillips: Yes, I do. There are new techniques and baits introduced every year. However, if you watch the types of lures that are consistently winning bass tournaments, you'll see that they're crankbaits, spinner baits, top-water baits, soft-plastic lures and jerkbaits. These baits may come in different colors and have various actions, but the tools are still the same. Also, you consistently can find more and bigger bass than other anglers when you fish for them in places where other fishermen aren't fishing, use lures that other fishermen aren't using (often old-timey lures) and fish harder, faster and longer than most other fishermen do. These are the characteristics of the men and the tactics in my book.

Question: John, what do you think has been one of your advantages for writing about bass fishing?

Phillips: I've written about bass fishing for more than 40 years, and I've been able to fish with some of the greatest bass fishermen who ever have lived. I interviewed all the Strike King professional fishermen for the Strike King webpage for many years. Because I posted their information daily, I had a tremendous amount of information and knowledge that I gleaned from these pros about how, where and with what to fish, under a wide variety of fishing conditions. But, more importantly, I learned the fishing philosophies of these great fishermen.

Question: John, give us some examples of different fishermen's philosophies that you admire.

Phillips: The way I really began to study the head games that are played in professional bass fishing was when I did an article on how an angler's mental attitude determines his success or failure as a bass fisherman. Rick Clunn was the first fisherman I know of who really began to study and expand the knowledge of the mental side of bass fishing, and he told me, "If I've done all my practicing for a major tournament up-river of the launch site, and as I take-off on the first day of the tournament a little still voice inside me says, 'Rick, you need to turn and go downriver to catch fish,' I don't try to reason with that intuitive message I've just received. I follow that little voice, and more times than not I'll have a good performance in that tournament. The mental side of the sport of bass fishing is the least-studied and the least-understood at this time."

As I watched Clunn in the early days of tournament bass fishing and saw him win four Bassmaster Classics and many-other tournaments and Angler-of-the-Year awards, I knew he was doing something different from the other fishermen. So, at a Bassmaster Classic, I picked the four men most-likely to win the tournament, and asked them two questions: "What will cause you to win this tournament," and "What can cause you to lose this tournament?" Every fisherman exactly predicted why they would lose, except one. When I interviewed Clunn, I asked, "Rick, how could you come to the Bassmaster Classic 2 days after fishing a tournament in the Arizona desert with temperatures over 100-degrees, and expect to win? You've got to be worn-out." "No, John, just the opposite is true," Clunn replied. "I've never been more prepared to win a tournament than I am at this Classic, and I expect to have one of my best performances ever in this tournament. I'm not tired. I'm invigorated. I've never felt like I've fished better than I'm fishing right now. All my lures and equipment are in the best condition possible. After performing well in Arizona, I've got a really-positive attitude going into this Classic. My body's conditioned to the heat and the long days of casting and winding, and I expect to have a great tournament at this Classic." Rick Clunn won the tournament.

Question: John, what do you believe the secret to Kevin VanDam's success is? He's one of the most-consistent winners of all the professional bass fishermen.

Phillips: I met VanDam at one of his first tournaments. He was about as cocky a teenager as I've ever seen. He was telling people like Rick Clunn, Larry Nixon and Roland Martin that one day he would beat them. I thought, "This kid must be out of his mind." But VanDam had learned a secret that very-few people understand. If you're going to do something great in life, you have to tell enough people that you'll do it, so that you can't back away from it. And, you have to work harder than the people who are already successful, if you're going to reach the same level of success that they have or a greater level of success. Kevin VanDam had something to prove. He also had and still has one-other personal characteristic that

151

gives him the edge: He has a burning passion, much like an addiction, to bass fishing. VanDam doesn't just like to fish for bass, he has an addiction to being the best bass fisherman who's ever lived. When he falls short of that expectation, he knows that tomorrow he'll have another day to get better. Although VanDam's a workaholic, practicing and competing in tournaments doesn't feel like work to Kevin VanDam. When he's on the water fishing, he feels like he's a little kid getting to play all day in his favorite sandbox.

Question: John, I've been to some of these bass-fishing seminars, and I've heard these pros talk about how they catch bass and the strategies they use, while not holding anything back. Aren't they afraid that the fishermen in the audience will take their ideas on methods and lures and compete with them?

Phillips: Rick Clunn gave me the best answer to this question that I've ever heard. "If I'm speaking to a group of 100 bass fishermen, and I tell them all the techniques they need to use to be successful, 50 of those 100 fishermen will begin to think in their heads about all the reasons that what I've just said won't work," Clunn says. "The other 49 percent of the people in the audience will try that strategy one time, and if it doesn't work, they won't use it again. But there'll be one person out of 100 who will try some of the tackle and techniques that I've taught about, and be successful using them. I'm not really concerned about that one person, because there are new people coming into competitive bass fishing every year, and they continue to get better and better. But I'm trying to get better and better also."

Another reason that the nation's best bass fishermen can teach their top methods for bass fishing at seminars and consumer shows and not worry about competition is that the one most-critical factor to catching bass on any day you fish is being aware of and adapting to the changes that take place on the water, while you're fishing. One of the best anglers to adapt to changing conditions during a fishing tournament is Kevin VanDam, who says, "When the sun goes behind a cloud, the fishing conditions have changed. When rain stops, the conditions have changed. When the water rises, falls, heats-up, cools-off, becomes more clear or more stained, or the wind blows or quits blowing, the fishing pressure increases or decreases, or there's a 2- or 3-degree temperature change, then you have to adapt your fishing to those conditions." I've observed VanDam in a tournament where he's come-in with the heaviest bag of fish caught that day after even a slight weather or water change by abandoning the places, lures and tactics he used to produce bass the previous day. He'll go to another part of the lake, use completely-different fishing tactics and lures he hasn't used in his pre-practice or during the tournament up until that time, and come-in from fishing that second day of the tournament with the heaviest limit of bass. The only way you can react to changes that quickly is by spending thousands and thousands of hours on the water, like VanDam and the other pros do.

Question: John, what is it you like about bass fishing and being with professional bass fishermen?

Phillips: I like bass fishing, because it's a sport I began to participate in when all I had to do was drop a minnow next to a log on a line attached to a cane pole, and fight the bass with that limber pole. Even through all the changes and the new technology that's been introduced to this sport, I still enjoy that tug on the line and that wild bass fighting for freedom when it comes out of the water and shakes its head. I like being around professional bass fishermen, because many of them are some of the best businessmen I've ever met and the great ones are gifted with a high degree of people skills. They're fun folks to hang-out with, and they've also been my teachers and my mentors.

Dedication

For more than 40 years, I've been interviewing and photographing professional bass fishermen, guides and the men and women who have caught world-record fish. This book is dedicated to the bass-fishing professionals who have given up their time, their knowledge and their wisdom to help make this book possible. The men in this book have shared their successes, their failures and the things they have learned about bass fishing with me for many years. So, thank you for not only being some of the top bass fishermen in the nation but for being my friend and being willing to share your bass-fishing knowledge with all of us.

Want more bass tips? Check out "How to Win a Bass Tournament: Personal Lessons from 8 Pro Bass Fishermen" and "Catch the Most and Biggest Bass in Any Lake: 18 Pro Fishermen's Best Tactics."

Like to fish for catfish and crappie? Get "Catfish Like a Pro" and "Crappie: How to Catch Them Spring and Summer."

Or, try my new sampler, "The John E. Phillips Sampler: Hunting, Fishing and More" for samples of books on other outdoor topics including deer, turkeys, saltwater fish and elk.

If you enjoyed this book, let us know by leaving a review on Amazon!

More Fishing and Hunting Books by John E. Phillips

Go to www.amazon.com/kindle, type John E. Phillips into Search and click on Author's Page (2nd choice) when it comes up to see books available, or go to www.nighthawkpublications.com, and on the left-hand side of the page, click on eBooks to learn more.

The 10 Sins of Turkey Hunting with Preston Pittman

13 Breakfast Recipes You Can't Live Without

13 Chili Recipes You Can't Live Without

13 Deer Recipes You Can't Live Without

13 Freshwater Fish Recipes You Can't Live Without

13 Saltwater Fish Recipes You Can't Live Without

13 Seafood Recipes You Can't Live Without

13 Soup, Chowder and Gumbo Recipes You Can't Live Without

13 Stew Recipes You Can't Live Without

13 Wild Turkey Recipes You Can't Live Without

Alabama's Inshore Saltwater Fishing: A Year-Round Guide for Catching More Than 15 Species

Alabama's Offshore Saltwater Fishing: A Year-Round Guide for Catching Over 15 Species of Fish

America's Greatest Bass Fisherman

The Best Wild Game & Seafood Cookbook Ever: 350 Southern Recipes for Deer, Turkey, Fish, Seafood, Small Game and Birds

Bowhunting Deer: The Secrets of the PSE Pros

Bowhunting the Dangerous Bears of Alaska

Catching Speckled Trout and Redfish: Learn from Alabama's Best Fishermen

Catch the Most and Biggest Bass in Any Lake: 18 Pro Fishermen's Best Tactics

Catfish Like a Pro

Courage: Stories of Hometown Heroes

Crappie: How to Catch them Spring and Summer

Deer & Fixings: How to Cook Delicious Venison

For Hot-Weather Fishing Success, Head to Reelfoot

Fishing Mississippi's Gulf Coast and Visitor's Guide

Hot-Weather Bass Tactics

How to Bass Fish Like a Pro

How to Become a Tournament Bass Fisherman

How to Find Your Elk and Get Him in Close

How to Fish Mississippi's Gulf Coast in June

How to Hunt Deer Like a Pro

How to Hunt Deer Up Close: With Bows, Rifles, Muzzleloaders and Crossbows

How to Hunt Turkeys with World Champion Preston Pittman

How to Make Money with Taxidermy: 70 Tips for Hunters and Small Businesses

How to Win a Bass Tournament: Personal Lessons from 8 Pro Bass Fishermen

Jim Crumley's Secrets of Bowhunting Deer

The John E. Phillips Sampler: Hunting, Fishing and More

The Most Dangerous Game with a Bow: Secrets of the PSE Pros

Moving Forward: Stories of Hometown Heroes

Outdoor Life's Complete Turkey Hunting

PhD Elk: How to Hunt the Smartest Elk in Any State

PhD Gobblers: How to Hunt the Smartest Turkeys in the World

PhD Whitetails: How to Hunt and Take the Smartest Deer on Any Property

The Recipes You Can't Live Without

The Recipes You Can't Live Without: Chilis, Stews, Soups, Chowders & Gumbo

The Recipes You Can't Live Without: Freshwater & Saltwater Fish & Seafood

Reelfoot Lake: How to Fish for Crappie, Bass, Bluegills and Catfish and Hunt for Ducks

Secrets for Catching Red Snapper and Grouper in the Gulf of Mexico

Secrets for Hunting Elk

The Turkey Hunter's Bible

Turkey Hunting Tactics

To buy my print books on hunting, visit: http://nighthawkpublications.com/hunting/hunting.htm. These books include:

Black Powder Hunting Secrets

Complete Turkey Hunting

Deer & Fixings

How to Take Monster Bucks

Jim Crumley's Secrets of Bowhunting Deer

The Masters' Secrets of Bowhunting Deer

The Masters' Secrets of Deer Hunting

The Masters' Secrets of Turkey Hunting

PhD Gobblers

PhD Whitetails

The Science of Deer Hunting

Turkey Hunting Tactics

For my fishing books, go to http://nighthawkpublications.com/fishing/fishing.htm. These books include:

Bass Fishing Central Alabama

Fish & Fixings

Masters' Secrets of Catfishing

Masters' Secrets of Crappie Fishing

Go to www.amazon.com and type in the names of our other print books to view them:

- The Turkey Hunter's Bible
- Crappie: How to Catch Them Spring and Summer

If you enjoyed this book, let us know by leaving a review on Amazon!

Made in the USA
San Bernardino, CA
13 July 2020